FORT WORTH'S
LEGENDARY
LANDMARKS

FORT WORTH'S
LEGENDARY
LANDMARKS

Photographs ❀ Byrd Williams

Text ❀ Carol Roark

TEXAS CHRISTIAN UNIVERSITY PRESS ❀ FORT WORTH

Copyright: 1995 Historic Preservation Council for Tarrant County, Texas

Roark, Carol E.
      Fort Worth's legendary landmarks: text by Carol Roark :
      Photography by Byrd Williams
      P.   cm.
      Includes Index.
      ISBN 0-87565-143-7
1. Historic buildings – Texas – Fort Worth – Pictorial works. 2. Architecture – Texas – Fort Worth – Pictorial works. 3. Fort Worth (Tex.) – Buildings, structures, etc. – Pictorial works. I. Title.

F394.F7R63 1995   95-7571
976.4'5315 – dc20   CIP
                                      Printed in Canada

Design / Margie Adkins

PREFACE

This volume presents a selection of Fort Worth's most architecturally and historically significant buildings, drawn from a list of resources identified during the course of the Tarrant County Historic Resource Survey, a ten-year project undertaken by the Historic Preservation Council for Tarrant County, Texas and its consultant, Page, Anderson & Turnbull, Inc., in the 1980s.

Buildings considered for inclusion in the book had to be:
- listed in the Tarrant County Historic Resources Survey
- located within the Fort Worth city limits on January 1, 1994
- built before 1945
- listed in or eligible for listing in the National Register of Historic Places or designated as either a Texas Recorded Historic Landmark or a City of Fort Worth Landmark (and not significantly altered since listed or determined eligible; determinations of National Register eligibility for some buildings have been made since the survey was completed)

A committee made up of historians, architects, and individuals active in historic preservation made the difficult choices about which buildings to include. Committee members tried to identify buildings that reflected a cross section of Fort Worth's neighborhoods, important historical time periods, building types, and architectural styles, but architectural quality was a deciding factor in all cases.

The photographs in this book were taken over a period of eight years by Byrd Williams. Working with large-format view cameras which produce negatives ranging from 5 x 7 inches to 18 x 24 inches, Williams practices a labor-intensive art requiring substantial time and effort to produce each image. The photographs in this book are a combination of special images from Williams' files and new work commissioned for this project. As a result the images document Fort Worth's historic buildings over an extended period of time.

ACKNOWLEDGEMENTS

No work is a solitary endeavor, and this project owes much to members of the Fort Worth historic preservation community and to fellow scholars, librarians, and historians. The Amon G. Carter Foundation and The Summerlee Foundation provided generous support for completion of the manuscript and photographs for this volume, as well as for the production of the book itself. The project would not have been possible without the support of the Historic Preservation Council for Tarrant County and its ongoing commitment to document our community's rich architectural heritage. Files compiled as part of the Tarrant County Historic Resources Survey were the basis for much of the information in this book.

The building selection committee included Paul Koeppe, Susan Campbell, Marty Craddock, Bob Adams, Jane Cranz, Deborah Phelan, Quentin McGown, Robin Reynolds and myself. Karl Komatsu, Reba Henry, and

DOWNTOWN FORT WORTH

Judy Cohen, whose book *Cowtown Moderne* provided invaluable information about Moderne buildings and their architects, also provided thoughtful input. My thanks go to these individuals for their efforts in this exhilarating and difficult task.

Ellen G. Oppenheim, chair of the Historic Preservation Council's Publications Committee during 1994, provided much-needed advice and support. Ann Kimbrough, the council's volunteer coordinator, also deserves thanks for her logistical coordination and unfailing good humor. Judy Alter, of TCU Press, has been both a good friend and a motivating editor, and I appreciate her enthusiasm over the long haul.

Staff at historical organizations and libraries throughout the state have been extremely helpful in gathering information for this project. My colleagues in the Texas/Dallas History Division at Dallas Public Library — Michael D. Smith, Jimm Foster, Marvin Stone, John Cloninger, Sharon Van Dorn, Yolanda Okwah, Michael K. Smith and Robert Nelson — all deserve particular thanks for their patience as I took time off to work on the book as well as for the questions they answered and the general support they gave. Ken Hopkins, Tom Kellum, and Max Hill, local history and genealogy staff at the Fort Worth Public Library, also provided invaluable assistance and never flinched at my repeated questions. Likewise, Gerald Saxon, Marcelle Hull, Betsey Hudon, Sally Gross, and other staff members in Special Collections at the University of Texas at Arlington Libraries were always eager to help me track down elusive bits of data. Texas Historical Commission staff, including Linda Roark, Della Keeshan, Ruben Moreland-Ochoa, Cynthia Beaman, and Tere O'Connell, responded to my many requests for National Register or Texas Historical Marker nominations. Sue McCafferty, executive director of the North Fort Worth Historical Society, provided information or gave me leads on several North Side landmarks. A special thanks goes to Rynda White Lemke as well as to Daryl Robbins, Erin Miller, and James Dorrel for their help with the photographs. City of Fort Worth employees who ably assisted me included Julia Hertenstein, Martha Chambers, Tennie Cole, B. Don Magness, Charlie Angadicheril, Jolene Loftis, Patsy Smith, Ann Kovich, and Becky Borton.

Those who own, live in, work with, or have a family involvement with the buildings listed in this book also provided invaluable assistance. They include Kate Singleton, Kay Fiahlo, Ruby Schmidt, John Shiflett, Christi Stanley, Kenneth and Sherrie Pounds, Robert Nicolais, Muriel Allen, Fred Ballinger, Susan Smith, Jane McAleavey, J'Nell Pate, Lorenza Moore, Jackie DeBolt, Vicki Dickerson, Jean Trager, Betty Shuler, Barbara Willis, and Armentha Hill.

Byrd Williams and I have worked together on several projects over the years, and I am pleased that we were able to collaborate on this endeavor. I treasure Byrd's magnificent images, his easy-going professionalism, and his friendship.

Carol Roark
December 4, 1994

STAR ON MAIN STREET

INTRODUCTION

The buildings in which we live our daily lives tell us about the forces that shape the growth of our community and the visionaries who transformed their dreams into viable institutions. Although Fort Worth has the trappings of any major metropolitan city – shopping malls, suburbs, and office towers – it is enriched by the many buildings that reflect its colorful and diverse heritage. Some of these buildings – like Louis Kahn's Kimbell Art Museum (1969-1972), Paul Rudolph's Texas Commerce Bank Tower and City Center Tower II (1982 and 1984), or Fay Jones' Marty Leonard Chapel built for the Lena Pope Home (1990) – are contemporary structures that have received national acclaim. This book focuses on Fort Worth's historic buildings (those built before 1945) whose design and background reflect earlier periods of the city's history but whose stories are not as well known today.

While Fort Worth is relatively young in comparison even to other Texas communities, its early history rivals more notorious western frontier towns for wide-open excitement. Successive redevelopment, courthouse fires, and neglect have all taken their toll on the record of the town's first years, however, leaving us with much legend and relatively few hard facts. No structures survive from the old fort, founded in 1849, and very few pre-railroad era buildings weathered repeated efforts to upgrade and modernize the city's infrastructure. An 1853 report documenting the condition of the fort's log and wood-frame buildings when the army abandoned the post notes that almost all were "leaky." Although the civilian population made use of these buildings in the short run, they were demolished or converted to storage use as soon as more comfortable accommodations were available.

Virtually all of the pre-1876 buildings in Fort Worth were wood-frame structures clustered near the stone courthouse within a few blocks of Main Street. Most of the wooden commercial structures were replaced by more substantial brick or stone buildings in the decades following the arrival of the railroad, but a few residences have survived. Some are at the core of what are now larger houses, but two early homes – one folk cabin and one Italianate house – give a flavor of the town's early dwellings.

The Van Zandt Cottage was remodeled and somewhat romanticized in 1936, but its small size and functional simplicity are traits common to many houses built in and around Fort Worth during the 1860s and early 1870s. Constructed without formal plans, these houses followed traditional practices that evolved to meet climactic and family needs. The central hall (now enclosed) and shed-roofed porch (originally the house had a shed-roofed porch on one facade and a full, continuous-roofed porch on the other) provided shelter from the hot summer sun, while shed additions (in this case added during the 1936 renovation) allowed for economical enlargement.

The Bennett-Fenelon House, on the other hand, was probably built from a printed plan book. Nationally, the popularity of the Italianate style was in general decline following the financial panic of 1873. In 1875, as Fort Worth anticipated the arrival of the railroad, such a house might have been a logical choice for a merchant who planned to capitalize on the opportunities the rail line would bring. Smaller than many of the homes built after the arrival of the railroad, the Bennett-Fenelon House is one of the earliest local residences to reflect an interest in style rather than in mere functionality.

After 1876, the prosperity brought by the railroads enhanced Fort Worth's interest in architectural trends. Improved finances and a dependable transportation connection made a wider variety of building materials available, and the promise of greater economic stability attracted businessmen who built new shops, offices, and residences. Population growth also sparked the need for schools, churches, and civic buildings. James J. Kane, the city's first architect, arrived in 1876, and at least two of his buildings – St. Patrick Cathedral and St. Ignatius Academy – still stand.

Although many of Fort Worth's nineteenth-century buildings have been demolished or remodeled to the point that they have lost their architectural integrity, there are remarkable survivors which offer a idea of the many fine buildings the post-railroad building boom spawned. Some of the buildings described here are contained within the central business district, but others push out to the city's first suburban neighborhoods (today they would be considered inner-city) – Quality Hill, the South Side, and Arlington Heights.

While these buildings are too few in number to present a complete catalog of nineteenth-century architectural styles, they do represent trends popular in the rest of the country – even though Fort Worth's examples were often constructed a few years later than similar structures on the East Coast. The best surviving nineteenth-century commercial structure is the Land Title Block, built in 1889 to house various real estate operations including the Chamberlin Investment Company which developed Arlington Heights. Two stories high, the eclectic brick, sandstone, and glazed-tile Victorian building was typical of Fort Worth's commercial streetscape during the 1880s.

Churches and schools built during this period generally followed traditional styles. J. J. Kane designed St. Patrick Church in the well-established Gothic Revival style, but he chose to draw plans for St. Ignatius Academy in the somewhat more secular – and, by 1888, out of date – French Second Empire style. He may have been responding to the wishes of the Sisters of St. Mary of Namur, a Belgian order whose European background might have made them sympathetic to the style. Fort Worth's oldest remaining public school, Stephen F. Austin Elementary School, is a handsome and stately Romanesque Revival building.

Beaux Arts architecture, favored for public buildings because of its grand scale and impressive detailing, was used for the Tarrant County Courthouse and Santa Fe Depot. Both structures were designed to impress both first-time visitors and the local citizenry and give them a sense of Fort

Worth's growing status. Sited on the bluff overlooking the Trinity River at the north end of the central business district, the courthouse remains the community's most prominent historical landmark while continuing to serve as a primary facility for court and records services.

During the last quarter of the nineteenth century, Fort Worth's residential development began to move out of the central business district. Bluff-top lots overlooking the Trinity River were chosen by many well-to-do residents for the breezes that cooled the property during the hot Texas summers, and Arlington Heights developers hoped that their elevated location would also prove popular. Large Victorian homes built in these neighborhoods include the Chateauesque-style home of William Bryce in Arlington Heights and the Queen Anne-style Eddleman-McFarland and Pollock-Capps residences on Penn Street. Architect Marshall R. Sanguinet's own Arlington Heights home did not follow the historical and ornamental precedents of the Victorian era. He initially designed a pure Shingle-style house – an original American form – which relied on an irregular plan and a covering of wooden shingles for its appeal rather than on elaborate detailing. Sanguinet rebuilt the house with a brick first story following an 1893 fire and later made other changes to accommodate his family, but at the time it was built the house was one of the most innovative and modern residences in Fort Worth.

The South Side, south of the Texas and Pacific railroad tracks, also began to develop during this period, but many subdivisions platted during the 1880s and 1890s were not fully developed until the streetcar lines began service to the area after 1900. Nineteenth-century homes built in this middle-class area took advantage of balloon-frame construction techniques, which made it easier to build houses with irregular floor plans. These houses also exhibited extensive decorative detailing. Machine-produced moldings, doors, and trim were easily added to any house, and what is frequently called Victorian gingerbread trim became very fashionable This trend is notable on small cottages such as the Keith-Peace House as well on somewhat larger residences like the

ST IGNATIUS ACADEMY

Benton House, which is the best remaining Victorian cottage in Fort Worth.

Fort Worth had long been a center for cattle-related activities, but the establishment of the Fort Worth Stock Yards Company in 1893 and the opening of the packing plants in 1902 solidified the city's position as a trading center for West Texas ranchers. Fort Worth was "the big city," and many well-to-do West Texans built homes and established business offices here. The successful packing plants also needed workers – and many immigrants made their way to Fort Worth to establish new lives. A good number settled on the North Side which, although it was platted in 1888 by New York landscape architect Nathan Barrett as the town of North Fort Worth (annexed by Fort Worth in 1909), did not develop until after the packing plants arrived. The homes and institutions of the North Side reflect the diverse cultures that contributed to the success of the stockyards and packing plant operations.

Local architecture during this period was influenced not only by the packing plants' infusion of cash into the community's economy, but also by changing tastes which shifted away from the ornate Victorian styles towards simpler designs. Industrialization spurred the acceptance of functional designs based on operational efficiency rather than aesthetic concerns.

This trend can be seen most clearly in the buildings associated with the stockyards and packing plants. The examples in this volume include the Swift & Company Office Building, the Live Stock Exchange, and the Coliseum. Of the three, the Mission Revival-style Live Stock Exchange is the most elaborate structure. Drawing on southwestern Hispanic traditions – stucco construction, courtyard, arcaded entry porch, and Mission-shaped parapets – it has a strong regional identity, appropriate for a facility serving the livestock industry. The Coliseum is also a handsome Mission Revival structure, but the design focuses on the facility's function as a show arena. Originally Swift & Company's office building was a spare and functional structure but, with its adaptive reuse as a restaurant, the colorful paint job on the two-story wooden gallery and interior remodeling give the building a richer air.

Both North Fort Worth and Fort Worth grew rapidly during this period. Downtown, new "skyscrapers" were erected with steel-frame construction and elevators. Some, like the seven-story Flatiron Building, did not retain the title for long as taller neighbors were built. The Neoclassical Burk Burnett Building, a typical base-shaft-capital skyscraper form, has twelve stories with an ornamental terra cotta capital that resembles a confectionery delight.

New churches were organized to meet the needs of an expanding population, and a number of established congregations built larger buildings. Most were still located in the central business district and followed traditional styles for ecclesiastical architecture including Gothic Revival (St. Andrew's Episcopal and Allen Chapel African Methodist Episcopal), Neoclassical (Mount Gilead Baptist), and Renaissance Revival (First Christian). The first suburban churches were also built during this period to provide a place of worship closer to home. Saint Demetrios Greek Orthodox Church chose the Byzantine style for its North Side church, an appropriate design given the national origin of its members, but unusual in Fort Worth. Missouri Avenue Methodist Church, an early South Side suburban church, selected a more eclectic design—a vaguely Prairie-style form with Sullivanesque and Gothic detailing.

Residential architecture during this period included a wide variety of styles. Some drew their inspiration from the ornate Victorian styles of the nineteenth century but most reflected a growing interest in less cluttered forms The 1904 Maxwell-Liston House is closer in spirit to the circa 1899 Garvey-Veihl House and the Victorian mansions of Quality Hill than it is to the Dutch Colonial Revival-style Talbott-Wall House built in 1903. More than one observer has wondered whether the 1908 Reeves-Walker House was designed by the architect who planned the 1899

Eddleman-McFarland House but, since Howard Messer returned to England about 1905, the possibility is unlikely. Nonetheless, the two houses are similar in many respects.

Many of the more "modern" houses built in Fort Worth during the two decades before the first World War were bungalows The designs were taken from plan books and several basic forms were reproduced with infinite variety in detailing. While few of these houses are outstanding in and of themselves, their architectural quality as a group is extremely important. The Fairmount/Southside National Register Historic District contains one of the largest and best-preserved collections of bungalows in Texas, but other examples may be found throughout the neighborhoods developed during this period.

Although larger than most bungalows, the Harris House, built from plans developed by the Craftsman designer Gustav Stickley, represents the more modern trend in architectural styles as do the Prairie-style Harrison-Shannon and Dillow houses. Period Revival styles that drew on a variety of historical architectural designs also started to become popular during this period. The Colonial Revival style was one of the most popular during this period because of its uniquely American background. The Dutch Colonial Revival-style Talbott-Wall House and Georgian-style Thistle Hill are good contrasts in the range of size, style, and materials used in Colonial Revival designs. Neoclassical styles, represented by the Williams-Penn and Ryan-Smith houses, also had a growing popularity.

The 1920s brought another dimension to Fort Worth's economic prosperity, Ties with West Texas established by the cattle industry were strengthened during the oil boom. West Texans had always thought of Fort Worth as their major city. When oil money began to flow, a good portion was pumped into the Fort Worth economy. Oil companies opened offices and refineries here, and many oil-rich ranchers and farmers moved to Fort Worth. The town's population grew from 106,482 in

1920 to 163,477 by 1930 – spurring a major effort to build new office towers and other buildings that would make the city look like the regional center that it was becoming. Many community institutions also prospered, and new meeting halls, houses of worship, and service facilities were built.

Architectural designs that drew inspiration from historic styles became prevalent in Fort Worth during the 1920s. Even modern commercial structures such as the W. T. Waggoner Building – which was advertised as thoroughly up-to-date – showed Period Revival motifs in its detailing. Others, such as Cook Children's Hospital and the Masonic Home Administration Building openly embraced historic Period Revival designs. Colonial Revival styles remained popular, as evidenced by the Georgian-inspired Hotel Texas and Elk's Lodge/YWCA, even in eclectic combination with motifs from other periods or the constraints imposed by the need to design a large hotel. Churches, notably St. Mary of the Assumption Catholic and First Methodist, continued to follow traditional historical styles for their buildings.

Residential architecture during this period is typified by both substantial and moderately-sized houses, mainly designed in Period Revival styles. Neighborhoods were further from the city center and were reached by automobile as well as by streetcar. While most of the examples listed in this volume are larger, architect-designed homes, the overall quality of residential design in Fort Worth during this period was quite good. Many neighborhoods which developed or grew largely during the 1920s, including Arlington Heights, Monticello, Oakhurst, Meadowbrook, Rivercrest, Berkeley, Park Hill, Ryan Place, University Place, and Mistletoe Heights, have hundreds of examples of well-designed Tudor, Mediterranean, and Colonial Revival houses.

Tudor Revival, with its steeply-pitched roofs and decorative half-timbering, was undoubtedly the most popular residential style in Fort Worth during the 1920s and 1930s and is represented

here by the Landreth-Davis, Lackey, and Leonard houses. Two Elizabeth Boulevard residences –
the Mediterranean Revival Dulaney House and the Spanish Colonial Revival Fuller-Snyder House
– evoke the historic architecture of the lands bordering the Mediterranean. Other notable examples of Period Revival houses include the Colonial-style King-McFadden-Dupree House, the
Flemish-style Gartner House, and the Romanesque-style Hanger House. Some residences, such as
the Freese and Parker houses, combine the form and detail of several styles to present a pleasing,
if not entirely historically accurate, design.

A few structures built with oil-boom money look forward rather than backward for their design.
Art Deco or Moderne architecture was inspired by a 1925 Paris exhibition of decorative and
industrial art that encouraged original designs which met a practical need. Although some design
forms from historical styles remained, they were streamlined and refined through a filter that
included avant-garde art, experiments with industrial fabrication techniques, and popular cul-
ture. This "modern" style appealed to those who wanted Fort Worth to look like a contemporary,
up-to-date city. The Blackstone Hotel and the Sinclair Building were both touted as modern
buildings equal to any of the new designs being built on the East Coast, and they span Fort
Worth's transition from the oil boom of the 1920s to the hardscrabble years of the 1930s.

Fort Worth's building efforts during the Depression were characterized by a substantial degree of
public-private cooperation and the use of both historic Period Revival and Moderne styles. In
1928 the chamber of commerce outlined a ten-point, Five Year Work Program designed to make
$100 million worth of improvements to Fort Worth's infrastructure. Projects already in the
pipeline at the time of the stock market crash helped blunt the impact of financial collapse during the first years of the Depression, and in later years federal work relief construction projects
took up the slack. The program's number one goal – the construction of a union depot facility –
was realized with the completion of the Texas & Pacific Passenger Terminal and Warehouse com-

UNITED STATES POST OFFICE

plex in 1931. The Texas & Pacific Railway constructed the stunning Zig Zag Moderne terminal and freight warehouse buildings and relocated track, while the City of Fort Worth undertook a major grade separation and street improvement project.

Other projects from the early 1930s involved Period Revival-style buildings: the federally-funded Beaux Arts-style United States Post Office, the Spanish Colonial Revival addition to the city's North Holly Water Treatment Plant, and the privately-constructed Spanish Colonial Revival-style Public Market Building. During the mid-and late-1930s, Fort Worth used work-relief monies to fund a large school renovation and construction project, and most of the designs were Period Revival styles. Lily B. Clayton Elementary School is a good example of the buildings this program built.

The Moderne style has, however, become almost synonymous with civic architecture during the 1930s because it was used for so many publicly-funded projects. Fort Worth boasts an extraordinary collection of Moderne public structures including the United States Courthouse, North Side Senior High School (the only Moderne-design school built), Farrington Field, City Hall/Public Safety and Courts Building, and the Will Rogers complex. The Masonic Temple, which was designed in the Classical Moderne style to save money, is – nonetheless – an excellent example of the style and must be added to Fort Worth's impressive list of commercial and public Moderne structures.

Despite the presence of these buildings, the Depression years had a strong impact on Fort Worth. Fewer structures were built, and many projects involved additions (North Holly Water Treatment Plant and Lily B. Clayton Elementary School) or renovations (Holy Name/Our Mother of Mercy Catholic Church) rather than new construction. New houses were built, but they tended to be smaller than those erected during the 1920s, Most, such as the Mack-Ellman House, were Period

Revival designs, although Fort Worth does have a few Moderne residences. The most notable of these is the Streamline Moderne house designed for Charles M. Davis, an engineer who built his own home as well as several other smaller rental properties.

Folk houses, styles that were popular for generations and built largely without formal plans, were still built in Fort Worth during the 1930s. The earliest surviving residence, the Van Zandt Cottage, is a folk house as are the most recent homes included in this book – the shotgun houses located at 930-942 East Oleander Street. In between are buildings which reflect the success of Fort Worth's major industries, the largess of its benefactors, and the brick-and-mortar responses the community made to the forces that shaped its history. ⊗

THE FRONTIER · Pre-1875

No structures survive from the original Fort Worth, and very few pre-railroad era buildings – most of which were wooden structures – escaped the later drive to build permanent structures of brick or stone in the expanding central business district. Although the physical evidence of this time dominated by cattle drives and wide-open living is slim, the romantic notion of Fort Worth as a rough and ready "Cowtown" continues to energize the city.

The Van Zandt Cottage is reputedly the only cabin in Fort Worth still standing on its original site. Located on the north side of what was called the Old Weatherford Road – which saw service as a cattle trail and stage road – the cottage is now on the western edge of Trinity Park. An exact construction date for the cabin is not known, and because the Tarrant County Courthouse burned in 1876, destroying deed records, even the early ownership of the property is unclear. It appears that Sarah M. and George Scoggins of Brazos County bought the tract of land on which the cabin stands in 1866. Major Kleber Miller Van Zandt (1836 - 1930), the person most closely associated with the structure, acquired the property about 1870 or 1871 after he filed suit against Scoggins for unpaid debts owed to his mother, Mrs. Isaac Van Zandt, Sr. The suit forced sale of the property at auction, and Van Zandt purchased it, probably with the cabin already constructed.

K. M. Van Zandt and his family settled in Fort Worth in December 1865. Trained as a lawyer, Van Zandt never practiced in Fort Worth, but followed business opportunities including banking, retail merchandising, and the cattle business. It is not clear whether Van Zandt and his family ever lived in the cabin, but local legend places them there between about 1871 and 1878. By the 1880s, the Van Zandts were living at the corner of Penn and West Seventh streets. It is also possible that they may have used the adjacent property as a tenant farm

The Van Zandt Land Cattle Company still owned the site in the early 1930s. When plans for the celebration of the 1936 Texas Centennial were made, the Board of Control of the Fort Worth Frontier Centennial allocated $2,000 to the Women's Division for the restoration of the cottage, so that it could be opened to the public in conjunction with the Centennial celebration. This group coordinated the project with assistance from the Julia Jackson Chapter No. 141 of the United Daughters of the Confederancy and the Daughters of the Republic of Texas.

The appearance of the cottage today dates from the 1936 rehabilitation rather than its original nineteenth-century look. Photographs taken of the deteriorated cabin just prior to the renovation indicate that it was probably originally a two-room, dog-trot cabin with an open, roofed passageway between the rooms that was later enclosed to form a central hall.

During the renovation, architect Joseph R. Pelich replaced the rough, feather edge clapboard siding with a more uniform siding that was painted gray. Small windows were replaced by larger ones, and shutters were added. A large porch on the north side of the house was enclosed to form a small room, a dining room, and a kitchen. The foundation of the original detached kitchen can still be seen behind the house, but the structure had long since disappeared by 1936. A new small back porch and bathroom were built, and the small, narrow porch on the front of the house was replaced by a wide, columned porch running the full length of the house. Although the cottage does not look as it did during the nineteenth century, Pelich's alterations are now over fifty years old and are significant as an early attempt to preserve Fort Worth's frontier heritage. ❦

BENNETT-FENELON HOUSE • 731 SAMUELS AVENUE •c.1875

*S*amuels Avenue, named for Baldwin L. Samuel (1803 - 1879), a former gold miner and farmer, is one of Fort Worth's oldest remaining residential streets. In 1870, Samuel bought the old Nat Terry farm north of town along the bluff overlooking the Trinity River. Residential development grew along the road that led from downtown Fort Worth to Samuel's home and the street soon bore his name.

Trail drivers brought herds of cattle close to Samuel's property, passing just east of Pioneer's Rest Cemetery at the southern end of Samuels Avenue.

Among the businessmen who built homes on Samuels Avenue during the 1870s was David C. Bennett, a dry goods merchant who later served as vice-president of First National Bank. According to city directory records, Bennett and his wife Mildred lived here from about 1875 until 1910. The house is the oldest surviving house on Samuels Avenue and one of the oldest in Fort Worth. Many of the smaller wood-frame homes built before the railroad arrived in 1876 were torn down so that commercial buildings could be erected. The fact that only two families have owned the Bennett-Fenelon house probably helped ensure its survival.

Thomas P. Fenelon, a city passenger agent for the Gulf, Colorado and Santa Fe Railway, moved into the house in 1915 and purchased it from Mildred Bennett in 1920. Various members of the Fenelon family have lived here through the years, and the house remains in the Fenelon family.

The Bennett-Fenelon House is a two-story Italianate residence. The style was popular in the Northeast and Midwest, as well as in San Francisco, but was less common in Texas. Typical elements of the style present here include a hipped roof, wide eaves supported by decorative brackets, and prominent bracketed lintels over the windows. The front porch probably dates from the turn-of-the-century because the design is inconsistent with the Italianate style, and the two-story addition to the rear was also built at a later date. ❦

Revival designs, although Fort Worth does have a few Moderne residences. The most notable of these is the Streamline Moderne house designed for Charles M. Davis, an engineer who built his own home as well as several other smaller rental properties.

Folk houses, styles that were popular for generations and built largely without formal plans, were still built in Fort Worth during the 1930s. The earliest surviving residence, the Van Zandt Cottage, is a folk house as are the most recent homes included in this book – the shotgun houses located at 930-942 East Oleander Street. In between are buildings which reflect the success of Fort Worth's major industries, the largess of its benefactors, and the brick-and-mortar responses the community made to the forces that shaped its history. ⊛

BENNETT-FENELON HOUSE

THE TARANTULA NETWORK • 1876 – 1901

The Texas & Pacific Railway's 1876 arrival in Fort Worth and the later location of other railroad lines in Fort Worth had a tremendous impact on the town's stability and business growth. Cattle could be shipped rather than driven to market, and other goods – including building materials – became more readily available. Fort Worth promoter and newspaper editor B. B. Paddock envisioned a network of rail lines centered in Fort Worth that looked like a tarantula spider. His dream was fulfilled, and the arrival of the railroads spurred Fort Worth's first major building boom.

Sitting alone on a square city block, the Land Title Block is Fort Worth's best surviving nineteenth-century commercial building. The small Victorian Romanesque structure showcases a rich variety of materials including pressed red brick, red sandstone, multi-colored glazed brick, cast iron, and stained glass. A panel depicting a tree, an owl, and a mockingbird with outstretched wings, reputedly the city's oldest surviving stone carving, graces the east end of the second floor. Architectural historian Blake Alexander notes that the Land Title Block is "one of the better examples of the brick mason's skill in using intricate brick patterns." Square bricks over the first floor windows form an "X" and "O" design.

The building was built by the Land Mortgage Bank of Texas, which had its offices on the first floor. Haggart and Sanguinet, a forerunner of the important local firm of Sanguinet and Staats, designed the building. Other early tenants included the Chamerberlin Investment Company, which promoted the initial development of Arlington Heights, and the law firm of Ross, Heard and Ross, whose initials appear in a panel on the second floor of the building. Through the years, the building has housed banks, real estate and title companies, attorneys' offices, and cafes.

The interior, in particular, has been frequently altered to accommodate a variety of tenants, but the Land Mortgage Bank's safe is still in place on the first floor. The exterior retains many original elements including the multi-colored glazed brick on the first floor and fine stained glass windows upstairs. The Flying Saucer Beer Emporium leased the property in 1994. The Land Title Block was designated as a Recorded Texas Historic Landmark in 1977. ⊛

ST. PATRICK CATHEDRAL

LAND TITLE BLOCK

*L*ate nineteenth-century Fort Worth was largely a Protestant town, but the Catholic community was growing, enriched primarily by Irish immigrants who made their way west building railroad tracks and operating the lines. Father Jean M. Guyot, a native of France, came to Fort Worth to pastor St. Stanislaus Church, St. Patrick's predecessor, in 1884. Guyot recognized the need for a larger building – St. Stanislaus was a small wood-frame structure – and began to make plans for the construction of this church. Local architect James J. Kane (1822-1901) was selected to draw plans for the building. Kane had also designed Fort Worth's City Hall and the 1882 renovation of the Tarrant County Courthouse (both structures have been demolished) as well as the St. Ignatius Academy building which was erected next to St. Patrick in 1888-1889.

His plans called for a Gothic building constructed of rusticated or roughly-finished limestone blocks with twin towers flanking the triple-portal central entry. Paired stained glass windows alternate with stepped buttresses on the side elevations beneath clerestory windows. Construction began in the summer of 1888, and the cornerstone was laid on October 14 of that year. Determined to build the building without incurring a major debt, church leaders had work done as funds were available. As a result, St. Patrick Church,

named for the Irish saint who shared a homeland with many of the parishioners, was not completed until 1892. Today St. Patrick remains the oldest continuously-used church building in Fort Worth.

Few changes were made to the church until 1946-1947 when Monsignor Joseph Grundy O'Donohoe, who had been named pastor in 1940, decided to undertake an interior renovation. Stating that "nature abhors a straight line – God is the author of nature – therefore, God prefers baroque with its curvaceous lines flowing and graceful curves," O'Donohoe had many of the Gothic elements of the sanctuary removed or replaced. The interior was completely replastered, ceiling beams and window frames were grained in faux walnut, the apse dome was repainted, the main altar was changed, and a new communion rail and side altars were installed. H. I. Moreland was the general contractor for this project. Today, the church interior still reflects O'Donohoe's passion for the Baroque.

In 1954 St. Patrick became a co-cathedral, sharing the seat of the diocese with Dallas, and in 1956 the diocese purchased St. Ignatius Academy from the Sisters of St. Mary of Namur. Monsignor Vincent J. Wolf, who assumed the pastorate in 1956 following O'Donohoe's death, established a fund which paid for renovations to the cathedral complex. During his tenure the exterior of the church was painted white, and

new lighting and air conditioning were installed. St. Patrick became the cathedral of the Fort Worth diocese in 1969. Along with St. Ignatius Academy, St. Patrick was one of the first structures in Fort Worth to be recognized for its historic significance when it was designated as a Recorded Texas Historic Landmark in 1962.

In 1985 a number of changes were proposed for the cathedral, including construction of a ramp for wheelchair access and enlargement of the sacristy. James Patrick, a Dallas architect, drew plans for these alterations, and Fisher-Pearson served as general contractor on the project, which was modified to address concerns about the historical integrity of the building. That same year the St. Patrick complex, including the cathedral, St. Ignatius Academy, and a 1908 church rectory were listed in the National Register of Historic Places. The cathedral complex still houses a diverse and active congregation, and the landmark structures provide a visual anchor to the southern end of Fort Worth's central business district.

ST. PATRICK CATHEDRAL

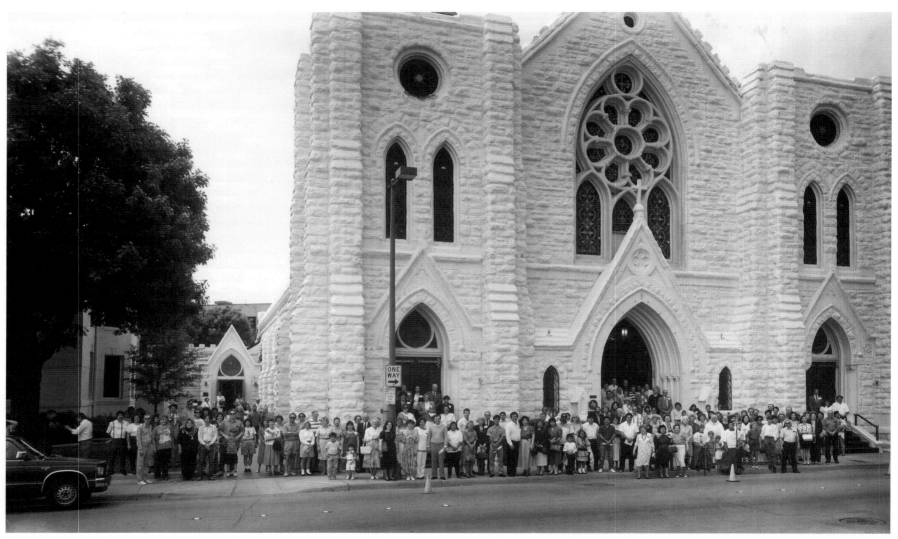

ST. PATRICK CATHEDRAL

*T*here had been a Catholic school in Fort Worth since at least 1881, but it was not affiliated with any particular order. In 1885, Bishop Thomas Gallagher of Galveston invited the Sisters of St. Mary of Namur to establish a new school in Fort Worth. Several sisters came from Denison and set up classes in a house near the site of the present building. By November 1888, the school had expanded to the point that a new structure was needed. The sisters borrowed $50,000 and commissioned James J. Kane, the architect who drew the plans for St. Patrick Church, to design this building for them.

Kane's striking Second Empire design, completed in time for fall classes in 1889, is the only surviving example of this style in Fort Worth. The three-story building, constructed of rusticated limestone blocks, has a mansard roof, dormers with arched hood moldings, decorative chimneys, and a belvedere or open roof-top tower. Colorful stained glass borders in the upper sashes of the tall, narrow windows are still largely intact.

Although the school was primarily an elementary school for most of its years, St. Ignatius did graduate several high-school classes of young women between 1904 and 1910 when upper-grade classes were moved to Our Lady of Victory Academy. This building was used for classrooms as well as for dormitory space. The school remained open as an elementary school until 1962. Since that time, the building has housed Sunday classes for the St. Patrick School of Religion and the parish hall.

Although the limestone walls have been painted white, the building still retains many of its original exterior characteristics. Inside, the original classrooms, chapel, and dormitory rooms have been modernized and adapted for contemporary use. Most of these alterations were made between 1972 and 1974. Like its neighbor, St. Patrick Cathedral, St. Ignatius Academy was listed in the National Register of Historic Places in 1985 and designated as a Recorded Texas Historic Landmark in 1962.

ST. IGNATIUS ACADEMY

11

FAIRVIEW/BRYCE HOUSE

*F*airview is one of the grand dames of Arlington Heights – a distinguished survivor of the failed nineteenth-century development that was the dream of Denver real estate entrepreneurs Alfred W. and H. B. Chamberlain. Although most residents think of Arlington Heights as an area that developed during the 1920s, there are at least five houses (see Sanguinet House) still standing today that were built between 1890, when the Chamberlains began to lay out Arlington Heights, and 1893, when they went bankrupt.

William J. Bryce (1861-1944), the man who built Fairview, would have had a natural interest in the Chamberlain development. For a bricklayer, the construction of large homes in this exclusive suburban area would have presented a good business opportunity. Bryce bought several lots from the Fort Worth Arlington Heights Land and Investment Company in 1892. His Chateauesque-style residence was designed by the firm of Messer, Sanguinet and Messer, architects who worked closely with the Chamberlains and who were responsible for almost all of the houses built in Arlington Heights during the early 1890s. Sanguinet and the Messer brothers also built their own homes in Arlington Heights. The Messers were British-born architects who practiced in Fort Worth for a short time. Howard Messer is best known for his design for the Eddleman-McFarland House, and Arthur Messer helped design the fanciful Texas Spring Palace exhibi-

tion hall. The Messers left Fort Worth shortly after the turn of the century, but Marshall Sanguinet became one of the state's best-known architects, practicing here in a succession of partnerships from 1883 until his retirement in 1926.

The Chateauesque style was popular during the late nineteenth century as a design appropriate for large architect-designed residences for wealthy and influential clients. While Bryce may not have quite achieved this stature at the time he built the house, the fact that he handled all of the brickwork on the solid brick structure probably made the use of such an imposing design possible. Bryce formed his own brick contracting business, and in later years he was successful in a variety of real estate and business ventures. Bryce also served as Fort Worth's mayor from 1927 until 1933.

The original design for Fairview has been altered through the years, primarily through the enclosure of porches, covering the original slate roof with shingles, painting the brick, and the construction of an additional porch on the west side of the house in 1946, but the picturesque design remains a pleasing composition. Both the carriage house and the original iron fence around the property still stand, although the carriage house has been converted for use as an apartment. Many of the changes, including the application of white paint which is slowly wearing away to reveal the original red brick, were made after Bryce's death. Although interior changes and additions have been made, the original hardwood floors and much of the wooden wainscoting and plaster trim are intact. Fairview was listed in the National Register of Historic Places in 1984 and designated as a Recorded Texas Historic Landmark in 1983.

*M*arshall R. Sanguinet (1859-1936), dean of Fort Worth architects, built this Arlington Heights house for himself and his family about 1894 from the ruins of his earlier home of the same design, constructed in 1890 but damaged by fire in 1893. When he built for the second time, Sanguinet used brick on the first floor exterior walls instead of shake shingles.

The original house was the first in the Arlington Heights development, an exclusive 'western' Fort Worth suburb which featured its own lake (Lake Como), hotel (Ye Arlington Inn), and an electric streetcar line running to downtown Fort Worth. Sanguinet, along with his English-born partners Arthur and Howard Messer, designed most of the twenty or so homes constructed in Arlington Heights between 1890 and 1893, when the Chamberlains went bankrupt following the Panic of 1893 and a fire destroyed Ye Arlington Inn.

As first built, the house was one of only a few Shingle-style residences constructed in Texas. Sanguinet was obviously fond of the style, for his firm designed several other structures, including the original River Crest County Club and the David Bomar/Amon G. Carter House, which drew on the Arts and Crafts movement and the Shingle style for their inspiration. Popular on the East Coast in the 1880s, the style was contemporary in that it did not rely on extensive decorative detailing for effect, but rather on an irregular profile clad in wooden shingles. Often the roof and walls were covered with the same type of shingles so that the surfaces seemed to be continuous.

Sanguinet enlarged the house in 1906, adding a Craftsman-style wood-paneled dining room to the west, enlarging the front porch and altering the columns, and constructing a porte-cochere over the driveway on the east side of the house. An enclosed back porch on the south side of the house and a sleeping porch above it (also now enclosed) were added at an unknown date. During this period the lot on which the house stood covered a city block. Portions were sold off over the years, but the home still sits on spacious grounds.

Sanguinet lived in the house with his wife, the former Edna Robinson, until his death in 1936. In 1940, on the fiftieth anniversary of the Arlington Heights development, Mrs. Sanguinet hosted a reunion at her home for members of the Pioneer Club, a group of women who had moved to Arlington Heights during its early days. Originally the women, who were three miles away from downtown Fort Worth linked only by a dirt road and the streetcar, met for one day every two weeks to socialize. Even after the area became more developed, they continued the tradition of all-day get-togethers. Mrs. Sanguinet remained in the house until 1948 when she moved to Dallas to live with her daughter. She died August 8, 1950, and the family sold the house in 1952.

The house has had several owners since the Sanguinets, and the interior has been remodeled to serve the needs of the families living there. The original iron fencing in front of the expansive lot has been preserved and contributes to the home's considerable charm. The Sanguinet House was listed in the National Register of Historic Places in 1983 and designated as a Recorded Texas Historic Landmark in 1981. In 1993, the home served as the Historic Preservation Council's Designer Showhouse. ⊛

STEPHEN F. AUSTIN ELEMENTARY SCHOOL/WILLIAMSON-DICKIE MANUFACTURING COMPANY HEADQUARTERS

*A*s Fort Worth grew in the late 1880s and early 1890s and residential neighborhoods outside the central business district were established, the local school system responded to the increasing number of students by building the Sixth Ward School in 1892 on Lipscomb Street only a few blocks south of the Texas & Pacific Railway tracks that marked the southern boundary of the downtown area. Strong residential development continued on Fort Worth's South Side as streetcar lines made a commuter lifestyle possible.

The building was designed by the local firm of Messer, Sanguinet and Messer (see Fairview and Sanguinet houses). The original school building was complemented by an almost identical mirror-addition to the north constructed in 1909. Sanguinet and Staats (Marshall R. Sanguinet and Carl Staats), successors to Messer, Sanguinet and Messer, designed the addition. In 1904 the name of the school was changed to Stephen F. Austin Elementary School, and it kept that designation until the school closed in 1977.

Both the original 1892 structure and the 1909 addition are constructed of red brick and rusticated or rough-cut limestone blocks. The two units are designed so that it appears as if the entire structure was constructed at the same time. A 1958 kitchen addition to the south of the main structure also uses similar materials and detailing. The Richardsonian Romanesque styling gives the building a solid and substantial feel. American architect Henry Hobson Richardson was the primary delineator of this style; popular from the 1870s through the 1890s and frequently used for public buildings, it features rounded arch entries, rusticated stone, windows grouped in a ribbon, and hipped roofs. The Stephen F. Austin Elementary School building is the purest surviving example of the style in Fort Worth (see also Land Title Block), but at one time it shared the stage with the old Federal Post Office and Courthouse and the old Texas and Pacific Union Passenger Station, both now demolished.

Williamson-Dickie Manufacturing Company, a leading producer of work and casual clothing, purchased the Stephen F. Austin Elementary School Building in 1980 and rehabilitated the structure for use as its corporate headquarters. Fort Worth-based Growald Architects handled the adaptive reuse project, which sensitively retained many original features of the building including the pressed tin ceiling, blackboards, and varnished wainscoting. The building was listed in the National Register of Historic Places in 1983. ⊛

*W*hen Major Ripley Arnold's scouting party first searched for a military post site "near the confluence of the Clear and West forks of the Trinity River," they chose a place on a bend in the river below the bluff. Returning about a month later, they established the fort on June 6, 1849. While the site had access to a good water supply at nearby Cold Springs, it was also close to the untamed river. Following a late-July flood, Arnold moved the post – named Fort Worth after his commander William Jenkins Worth who had recently died of cholera in San Antonio – to the top of the bluff overlooking the Trinity River.

The fort was laid out just north and west of the present courthouse site, the first in a series of blufftop developments. Tarrant County, named for General Edward H. Tarrant, a state legislator and Indian fighter, was established on December 20, 1849. When the army abandoned the fort in 1853, settlers who had been living near it moved into the buildings. Thus, Fort Worth had its beginnings on the bluffs, and the seat of county government has occupied this blufftop location for over 135 years.

After an 1860 election designating Fort Worth as the county seat, construction of the first permanent courthouse began on this site. The two-story stone building was only partially completed when the Civil War broke out, but it was finished after the war and served until destroyed by fire on March 29, 1876. Old stone blocks from the burned courthouse were used in the construction of a new building, a cross-shaped structure with a domed central axis. Despite an 1882 project to enlarge the building, the county grew so rapidly that by the early 1890s, the courthouse was again overcrowded.

In 1893 county commissioners allocated $500,000 to construct a new courthouse. Gunn and Curtiss (Frederick Gunn and Louis Curtiss) of Kansas City, Missouri, were selected to design the building. Probst Construction Company of Chicago was the general contractor for the project. Even though the new courthouse came in under budget – the final cost was $408,380 – Tarrant County citizens struggling to recover from the economic depression that began in 1893 were astounded at the high cost of the building and voted all of the commissioners out of office at the next election.

Gunn and Curtiss' design is a striking example of American Beaux Arts eclecticism, a classical style drawing inspiration from the buildings of the French and Italian Renaissance. As is typical of the style, the courthouse has entry porticos supported by paired Tuscan columns, paired Corinthian columns on the second level, a roof-line balustrade, and lavish stone carving. The building is constructed of granite from Burnett County and trimmed with marble from the same county. The central tower is topped by a copper domed lantern. Historian and newspaperman B. B. Paddock wrote that "it is claimed that the copper roof, glass in the windows and hardware are the only materials used in the construction of the building that are not products of Texas." It was a grand building, an appropriate symbol for what Fort Worth and Tarrant County wanted to achieve. Fittingly, the courthouse faced Main Street to the south – where most of the existing development had occurred – and the Trinity River and adjacent broad plains to the north. In the coming decade the North Side would provide the next major boost to the area's economy when the stockyards and packing plants were established.

The courthouse served faithfully until the early 1940s when major changes to both the interior and exterior were undertaken. Elevators, steam heating, and air conditioning were added, additional courtrooms were created by dividing two of the high-ceilinged district courtrooms with a mezzanine to provide two courtrooms in each space, and the rotunda was floored over covering the view of the dome from the first level. The original slate roof was replaced with copper in 1947, and during the 1950s the original revolving doors were removed and a 1,250-pound electrified metal American flag placed on top of the dome. A Civil Courts Building was constructed on the west side of the courthouse in 1957-1958. This building owes its current appearance to a 1988 project to create a trompe l'oeil (or "fool-the-eye") facade to match the 1893-1895 courthouse. Muralist Richard Haas designed the illusionistic facade.

Although there were occasional efforts to have the courthouse demolished and erect a "modern" building in its place, the structure has survived. In 1980 Tarrant County citizens approved a $3 million bond issue to restore the courthouse. Under the leadership of County Judge Mike Moncrief, the architectural firms of Ward Bogard and Associates and Burson, Hendricks & Wall Architects, Inc. were selected to head the restoration effort. Walker Construction Company was the general contractor for the project which was undertaken in 1983. This major rehabilitation effort blended restoration and renovation, rebuilding or replacing windows, cleaning the facade, and replacing one of the grand stairways and other details of the original courtrooms. Wiring, plumbing, and electrical systems were also updated, and some floor layouts were changed. The Tarrant County Courthouse was listed in the National Register of Historic Places in 1970 and designated as a Recorded Texas Historic Landmark in 1969. ⊛

LOOKING NORTH ON MAIN STREET FROM THE COURTHOUSE ROOF

TARRANT COUNTY COURTHOUSE

TARRANT COUNTY COURTHOUSE

21

*L*ucy "Lula" Foster Garvey (1857-1915), granddaughter of Baldwin L. Samuel for whom Samuels Avenue is named, and her husband William B. Garvey (1855-1915) bought this bluff-top lot from her parents, Mr. and Mrs. Isaac Foster, in December 1883. The couple soon built a small wood-frame cottage on the back of the lot facing the Fosters' residence next door. Garvey had a number of business enterprises. During the mid-1880s he was first a sand dealer, then a news dealer. In 1888 he entered the grocery business, operating a firm that became known as W. B. Garvey & Company, "dealer in staple and fancy groceries," and after 1900 he was active in fire insurance and real estate.

About 1899 the Garveys built a new, much larger home around the frame cottage, reorienting the front of the house towards Samuels Avenue. The two-and-one-half story house is a Free Classic adaptation of the Victorian Queen Anne style. Popular during the 1890s, these homes combine the inspiration of Elizabethan- and Jacobean-era design found in the Queen Anne style with the more classical elements of early asymmetrical Colonial Revival houses. The house sits towards the back of the large lot, but a fine original limestone retaining wall with gateway pedestals and wrought iron fencing runs along Samuels Avenue.

Sitting on a raised foundation of limestone blocks, the house has a typical asymmetrical Queen Anne form with a central hipped roof, which once had a widow's walk, and lower cross gables. Bracketed eaves, the circular corner tower with a bell dome, and the triangular gable detailing are also hallmarks of Queen Anne houses. The pedimented entry porch with Corinthian columns and the small second-story balcony of similar design are the primary Colonial Revival elements. The circular stairwell bay on the north facade has stained and leaded glass windows at the second-story level.

In his will, Mr. Garvey left the house and several other properties to Southwestern Baptist Theological Seminary, the Fort Worth Benevolent Home, and the Buckner Orphans Home in Dallas. These organizations sold the house in 1918 to Lena and Robert Veihl, a partner in the Veihl-Crawford Hardware store. Although Robert Veihl died in 1938, his wife continued to live here until her own death in 1958. The house had a succession of owners over the next fourteen years and was primarily used as a rental property.

By the time Brenda and Gordon Kelley purchased the house in 1972, it was in poor shape and facing condemnation. The Kelleys had a strong interest in historic preservation and made a commitment to stabilize and repair the house. With the assistance of their sons, the Kelleys did much of the work themselves. The Kelleys were also involved in the efforts to recognize and document the significance of the Samuels Avenue area. The house, which was designated as a Recorded Texas Historic Landmark in 1993 and as a City of Fort Worth Landmark in 1994, remains in the Kelley family .⊛

*T*he number of railroads providing service to Fort Worth grew dramatically during the 1880s and 1890s, and by the turn of the century the city felt the need for a new railroad depot to handle the increased traffic. Although the name of the architect is not known, this structure was built by the contracting firm of Smith and Bardon (David Smith and John Bardon) at an approximate cost of $50,000. When it first opened on March 1, 1900, the station served the Gulf, Colorado and Santa Fe and the Houston and Texas Central railroads. Other lines that operated out of the Fort Worth Union Depot, as the station was first called, included the Cotton Belt, Rock Island, Southern Pacific, and the St. Louis and San Francisco Railway (Frisco).

On February 21, 1901 at 5:00 a.m., a fire in the basement furnace rose to the roof, burning the wooden framework between the station roof and the metal ceiling. The roof collapsed, but the following day the *Dallas Morning News* reported that the building could "probably be restored with comparative ease, the walls, it is thought, being intact with little damage done outside of the roof." According to the newspaper, the station would remain open while repair work was done because the ticket office on the east side of the building was not damaged.

The Beaux Arts-style terminal is not as large or grandiose as some examples of the style, but it does have a wealth of detail including alternating bands of limestone and red brick on the ground floor, red and white diamond-patterned brickwork between the first and second stories and above the end windows on the second story, stone quoins (stones laid at the corners of buildings so that their faces are alternately large and small), and patera or circular ornaments flanking the four large arched windows on the second floor of the front facade. Iron eagles once topped the end parapet gables, but they have long since been removed. Overall, the play of red and white patterning enlivens the facade and makes the building one of the most distinctive in Fort Worth.

In 1938 the depot was renovated as part of an extensive program undertaken by the Fort Worth Union Passenger Station Company and the Santa Fe Railroad. "Modernization" was apparently the order of the day as the old brick portico was removed and replaced by the current projecting canopy and the interior was "redecorated and brought up to date." The station served several lines until 1960, when the Santa Fe became the sole railroad using the facility; the building was renamed the Santa Fe Depot. Amtrak operated passenger rail service out of the station between 1973 and 1995.

Inside, the main waiting room is two stories high with an arched or barrel-vaulted ceiling. Once painted in rich colors, the pressed metal ceiling and walls are now coated in a drab monochrome. Painted glass windows depicting the evolution of regional transportation from the Pony Express to steam locomotives were originally located in the three arched window openings on the north wall. They have been removed but are being preserved by a local museum. The marble flooring still remains, as do many of the decorative details.

The Santa Fe Depot was listed both in the National Register of Historic Places and designated as a Recorded Texas Historic Landmark in 1970. At this writing, it is one of the city's most endangered historic structures and adaptive reuse plans are urgently needed. ❀

SANTA FE DEPOT

SANTA FE DEPOT

SANTA FE DEPOT

27

*A*lthough this charming Folk Victorian cottage was built about 1898 for George D. Keith, a grocery salesman, it is best remembered as the residence of Joseph and Hazel Harvey Peace who purchased the house in 1939. The neighborhood, located on Fort Worth's near Southeast Side, was originally home to working class white residents such as Mr. Keith and James L. Jarvis, a foreman at the United States Helium Production Plant, who owned the house during the 1920s and 1930s.

The Peaces were among the first African-Americans to purchase a home in the area, and during the 1940s and 1950s it was a stable and thriving community for professional and middle-class families. Joseph "Joe" Peace was a contractor who built many houses, churches, and commercial structures in the neighborhood. His wife, Hazel, attended Fort Worth public schools before earning a bachelor's degree from Howard College and a master's from Columbia University. She returned to Fort Worth to teach English at I. M. Terrell High School, eventually becoming dean of girls and vice principal before she left in 1972 after almost forty years of service. Mrs. Peace's reputation at Terrell, the only area high school designated for African-American students before the school system was integrated, is legendary. She is remembered as a strict disciplinarian yet someone who inspired and motivated students to accomplish far more than they believed possible. After she left Terrell, Mrs. Peace worked for Bishop College in Dallas and served on several city boards and neighborhood councils.

Mr. and Mrs. Peace lived here for twenty years. After Joe Peace died in 1959, Hazel Peace moved down the street to her parents' old home, maintaining this structure as a rental property.

Although the L-form of the house is fairly simple, the delicate spindlework on the porch, bracketed window hood, patterned shingles in the gable, and original front door give the residence its delightful Folk Victorian style. At one time, there were literally hundreds of such cottages in Fort Worth, but demolition, inappropriate remodeling, and neglect have taken their toll. The Keith-Peace House is one of the best surviving examples of this extremely functional form. ❀

KEITH-PEACE HOUSE

29

POLLOCK-CAPPS HOUSE

*J*oseph Robert Pollock (c. 1851-1912), a homeopathic physician, moved to Fort Worth about 1887. During the years that Pollock practiced in Fort Worth, he built a considerable reputation for his medical skills and served three terms as the president of the Texas Homeopathic Physicians Association. Like many other successful late-nineteenth-century professionals in Fort Worth, Pollock turned to the bluff area overlooking the Trinity River when the time came to build his new home. In the days before air conditioning, bluff-top lots were valued for the breezes they caught – an important advantage during sweltering Texas summers. The area, including Penn Street and Summit Avenue (then called Hill Street), became known as Quality Hill. Pollock's house sits at the southern end of Penn Street on a dead-end cul-de-sac just north of the Lancaster Avenue Bridge.

The name of the architect who designed this Queen Anne Victorian home has not been confirmed, but local sources attribute the house to Howard Messer, who also drew plans for the Eddleman-McFarland House next door. The steeply pitched, irregular roof lines of the Pollock-Capps and Eddleman-McFarland houses are the only reminders of the many graceful Victorian homes that once abounded on Quality Hill. Like its neighbor, the Pollock-Capps House is one of Fort Worth's hallmark Victorian residences. Its asymmetrical form and varied materials – red brick, limestone, red and gray slate roofing, and copper finials – contribute to the home's picturesque charm.

In 1910, Pollock and his wife Phoebe sold the house to Sallie Capps, wife of attorney, real estate developer, and newspaper publisher William Capps, but the Capps occupied the home for only a few years. Their daughter Mattie Mae and her husband Frank M. Anderson lived in the house from about 1913 until her death in 1963, and her husband remained until 1971. During this time the house was remodeled, and some of its Queen Anne detailing was removed or obscured. The front porch was enlarged and rebuilt, two rooms were added to the back of the house, and the sleeping porch was enclosed. Frank Anderson sold the house to Historic Fort Worth, Inc. in 1971 in what was one of the first organized efforts to preserve a local landmark since the Van Zandt Cottage had been rehabilitated as part of Fort Worth's Texas Centennial celebration.

Architect Robert W. Chambers purchased the house from Historic Fort Worth, Inc. in 1974 with a deed restriction requiring a sensitive rehabilitation of the house. The front porch was restored to its original configuration and the interior adapted for use as office space. The property has had a number of owners since, and between 1990 and 1992 architect Bill Pruett undertook further remodeling and restoration work to provide offices for attorney Dwain Dent. Historic Fort Worth, Inc. secured a listing for the Pollock-Capps House in the National Register of Historic Places in 1972. The house was designated as a Recorded Texas Historic Landmark in 1977 and as a City of Fort Worth Landmark in 1991. ⊛

*T*his bluff-top Queen Anne style residence is the most intact Victorian home in Fort Worth. The fact that this remarkable landmark survives is due to the tenacity of Caroline (Carrie) Eddleman McFarland, who lived in the house from 1904 until her death in 1978. At a time when many other Quality Hill residences were falling to the wrecking ball, Mrs. McFarland decided to live in the house rather than sell and move elsewhere. Her decision also afforded protection to the Pollock-Capps House next door, because its single lot alone did not offer enough space for commercial development.

The house was built for wealthy Galveston widow Sarah C. Ball and her son Frank M. Ball. They reportedly moved to Fort Worth in order to be close to their next-door neighbor, Dr. Joseph R. Pollock, who served as the family's doctor. Howard Messer designed the home which was constructed at a cost of $38,000. The Balls did not live here for long — Frank Ball died in 1901 and his mother in 1904. The Balls' association with the house has dimmed with time, and today it is generally known as the Eddleman-McFarland House for the family that occupied the residence for the next three-quarters of a century.

William Harrison Eddleman purchased the house from Mrs. Ball's estate in December 1904. He came to Fort Worth from Weatherford to establish the Western National Bank, and his wife Sarah, daughter Carrie, and son-in-law Frank Hays McFarland moved into the house with him. At the time he moved to Fort Worth, Eddleman owned a controlling interest in twenty-six Texas banks. The Western National Bank failed in 1914, and Eddleman then became associated with the Denver Investment Company. After his wife's death in 1921, he gave the house to his daughter.

Frank Hays McFarland, a cattleman who ran polled herefords on his Parker County ranch, was one of the founders of the Southwestern Exposition and Fat Stock Show (now the Southwestern Exposition and Livestock Show). Carrie McFarland helped her husband keep the books and cattle registration records for the ranch, but she was also involved in local organizations. She was a founding member of the Fort Worth Day Nursery, which provided child care for working mothers, and the Assembly, a social group. Hays McFarland died in 1948, but Mrs. McFarland continued to live in and preserve the house for thirty years. Friends remember the poker parties that Mrs. McFarland hosted in the back parlor and recall that she had the house air-conditioned during the 1950s so that her poker-playing friends would not be uncomfortable.

Overall, the Eddlemans and McFarlands made few substantive changes to the house. The exterior, constructed of Pennsylvania pressed brick, sandstone, slate, and Georgian marble looks much today as it did when it was first built – save for a balustrade that was once present over the main entry porch and the shutters which are currently stored in the attic. The interior has patterned parquet floors, coffered ceilings, and walls paneled in oak and mahogany. Mrs. McFarland's major interior changes included new wall paper and light fixtures in some rooms, removal of most fireplace overmantels, and a general kitchen updating.

Carrie McFarland died on May 1, 1978 at the age of 100. In 1979 the house was purchased by the Junior League of Fort Worth with plans to preserve the house as it looked at the time of Mrs. McFarland's death. Restoration work, including a major reconstruction of the badly-deteriorated sandstone front porch in 1990-1991, has been carried out under the direction of John Volz of Volz and Associates of Austin. The Junior League transferred ownership of the house to Historic Fort Worth, Inc. in 1984. It currently houses Junior League offices upstairs, but the first floor is maintained as a house museum and is available for rental for special events. The Eddleman-McFarland House was listed in the National Register of Historic Places in 1979 and was designated as a Recorded Texas Historic Landmark and City of Fort Worth Landmark in 1980. ⊕

POLLOCK-CAPPS HOUSE & PORCH OF THE EDDLEMAN-MCFARLAND HOUSE

EDDLEMAN-McFARLAND HOUSE

33

EDDLEMAN-McFARLAND HOUSE

EDDLEMAN-McFARLAND HOUSE

*T*he Benton House is Fort Worth's most picturesque Victorian cottage. Sited on a large corner lot and still surrounded by its original fence, the one-and-one-half story Queen Anne-style residence was erected by Kansas City builder William Azro Benton for Benton's son Meredith Azro Benton (1861-1941) and his wife Ella Belle (1869-1942). M. A. Benton purchased three lots in the Fairmount Addition on July 3, 1900 for $375. Construction of the residence presumably began shortly thereafter.

Benton began his career selling tobacco in Indian Territory. By 1926, when he retired, Benton was a tobacco distributor for P. Lorillard and Co. He travelled frequently in the course of his business, and family accounts tell of Ella Belle Benton watching her husband's horse and buggy leave the old T & P Railway Station and cross the open prairie as he made his way home after a trip.

Mrs. Benton helped establish Fort Worth's public school kindergarten program and was instrumental in founding the Fort Worth Rose Society.

The house is built of cypress, and the Bentons' daughter recalled that all of the gingerbread trim was hand-sawn rather than machine-cut. The elaborate trim on the one-story porch, which wraps around the front and south sides of the residence, and the gingerbread trusses in the gables give the house its charming "wedding cake" appearance.

Originally, the Bentons built a large barn with a hayloft for their horses and a two-room servants' house on the west end of the lot. These structures were demolished and the current two-car garage and servants' residence constructed in 1937. The back of the main house, which is much simpler than the front facade, has a lattice-screened porch that once housed a cistern to collect rainwater for the family's use.

The Benton House has all the hallmarks of a Victorian Queen Anne cottage – an asymmetrical plan (thought to be more interesting visually than a symmetrical design), hipped roof with cross gables, spindlework, patterned wooden shingles, and a cutaway bay window. Inside, the layout groups the three bedrooms on the south side of the house and the parlor, dining room, and kitchen on the north. Most of the interior features, including fireplaces with oak mantels, transomed doors, and hardware with copper and bronze detailing, are original as well – and the Benton descendants, who still own the house, have made a special effort to preserve its historic character. The Benton House was listed in the National Register of Historic Places in 1981 and designated as a Recorded Texas Historic Landmark in 1978. It contributes to the Fairmount/Southside National Register Historic District and to the City of Fort Worth Historic and Cultural Sub-district, both designated in 1990. ⊛

KNIGHTS OF PHYTHIAS CASTLE HALL

*T*he first Texas lodge of the Knights of Pythias, a charitable, benevolent, and fraternal order, was established in Houston in 1872. Fort Worth's Queen City Lodge No. 21 was organized in 1877 and the Red Cross Lodge No. 14, in 1881. That same year their first meeting place was razed, and the two lodges conducted a subscription drive to purchase this lot at 315 Main Street, building their first castle hall on this site. The building, which was similar to the current structure, burned in 1901, but members were able to save the galvanized iron knight and place it in a niche on their new building.

The 1901 castle hall was designed by Marshall R. Sanguinet of the firm Sanguinet and Staats and built by contractors A. E. Newell and William Bryce. Reminiscent of a Flemish or Dutch medieval civic structure, the new hall had lease space on the first and second floors and meeting rooms for the Pythians on the third floor. This type of arrangement was common among fraternal orders because the rent received helped offset the costs of maintaining the building. Renfro Drug Company's Store No. 1 was located on the first floor from 1904 until 1939. Other tenants through the years included a veterinary surgeon, attorneys, real estate agents, and a number of physicians.

Groups affiliated with the Knights of Pythias, such as the Pythian Joint Relief Board, also had offices in the building. The Knights of Pythias had their strongest presence in Texas during the teens and twenties, when state-wide membership was about 30,000. Fort Worth knights have included George Gause, John P. Alexander, T. M. Gooch, Jr., Judge Marvin H. Brown, and E. M. Alvord. Lodge membership and tenant occupancy waned during the 1960s and early 1970s, and the Knights sold the building in 1975. Bass Brothers Enterprises acquired the building in 1978 and renovated it in 1981-1982 as part of the Sundance Square project. Woodward and Associates of Dallas were the project architects, and Thomas S. Byrne, Inc., general contractor, carried out the preservation project.

With its steeply-pitched slate roof, corner tower, stained glass window, and truncated side gables, the red brick castle hall is a distinctive, romantically-styled building. In 1976 the first knight was badly damaged in a fall as workmen attempted to remove him from the niche and transfer him to the new lodge hall, so the current suit of armor is a 1983 replica fashioned by the Astie Art Metal Studio of Dallas. The interior, which has been adapted for contemporary use, now houses retail, office, and theater space. The Knights of Pythias Castle Hall was listed in the National Register of Historic Places in 1970 and was one of the first buildings in Fort Worth to be designated as a Recorded Texas Historic Landmark, an honor the structure received in 1962. ⊛

KNIGHTS OF PHYTHIAS CASTLE HALL

LIVESTOCK EXCHANGE BUILDING

CATTLE AND CATTLE KINGS · 1901-1917

Cattle were big business in Fort Worth for most of the city's first century. Although the post-Civil War trail drives brought Fort Worth its reputation as a wide-open city and some measure of prosperity, local leaders envisioned a time when cattle would end their journey in Fort Worth, not simply pass through it. After several unsuccessful attempts to establish a local packing plant, victory finally came in 1902 when the Chicago-based meat-packing firms of Armour and Swift opened slaughterhouses and packing plants adjacent to the stockyards in North Fort Worth. The plants sparked a major development boom north of the Trinity River. Fort Worth reaped some of the benefits of this prosperity too, without having to suffer the smells of the stockyards, but nonetheless annexed North Fort Worth in 1909 and Niles City, which contained the Armour and Swift plants, in 1922 in order to harness the full economic benefit of local livestock operations.

For many years, the Livestock Exchange Building was the center of stockyards business operations, and today it continues to serve as the architectural and symbolic heart of the stockyards. Built to house the Fort Worth Stock Yards Company and livestock commission offices, as well as other associated businesses such as railroads that ran spur lines to the stockyards and the Stockyards National Bank, the Livestock Exchange Building was erected in 1902-1903 at the same time as the construction of the Armour and Swift packing plants. All cattle, hogs, sheep, mules, and horses sold in the Fort Worth Stock Yards were processed or cleared through the exchange. When the building opened for business in April of 1903, livestock pens stretched for acres around the building.

Located on Exchange Avenue, down the hill and just west of the packing plant operations, the Livestock Exchange Building is a classic example of Mission Revival architecture. Built of brick covered with rough-cast stucco, the two-story, U-plan building has a red tile roof, curving "Alamo" parapets, octagonal cupolas, and a one-story arcade which spans the space between the two wings of the building creating an entrance courtyard. Despite the stature of the building, the name of the architect is not known. According to historian B. B. Paddock, local brick contractor William Bryce built the building. There have been several additions to the back or north side of the building, but all were completed by 1915. Facade alterations, including the enclosure of a porch area in front, have been minor – and all early. Molly, the cast-metal longhorn centered in the main parapet who has become a icon for Fort Worth, was put up before 1905 and covers a clock niche.

In 1944, the building was sold to the United Stockyards Corporation. Following the decline in the local livestock and packing industries during the 1950s and 1960s, the condition of the building deteriorated significantly. Even so, it was designated as a Recorded Texas Historic Landmark in 1968. By the mid-1970s, with both the Armour and Swift plants closed and the economic underpinnings for the North Side in serious jeopardy, interest rose in historic preservation and tourism as a way to celebrate the cattle industry's legacy in Fort Worth and provide a stable business environment. In 1975, area residents formed the North Fort Worth Historical Society, which now has offices and a museum in the Livestock Exchange Building.

The Stockyards Historic District was listed in the National Register of Historic Places in 1976, and in 1977-1978 the Livestock Exchange Building was renovated under the direction of Thomas E. Woodward and Associates, architects. Entrepreneur Holt Hickman purchased the building in July 1994 as part of his plan to redevelop the stockyards area as an entertainment district. Hickman plans to rehabilitate the Livestock Exchange and continue to use it for offices. Although only a few livestock commission companies still have offices in the building, it continues to provide space for the museum as well as a number of professionals, businesses, and organizations. ❀

LIVESTOCK EXCHANGE BUILDING

45

SWIFT & COMPANY OFFICE BUILDING

*I*t made good business sense for Armour and Swift to locate their meat-packing plants closer to the area where cattle were raised. Together, Texas, New Mexico Territory, and Indian Territory produced twenty per cent of the cattle in the United States, and Fort Worth's offer to subsidize construction of the plants made the location even more attractive. According to J. Ogden Armour, his company was the first to plan to come to Fort Worth but offered Swift fifty per cent of the Fort Worth operations if Swift agreed not to build a competing plant in Dallas. In return, Armour was allowed to begin operations in St. Louis where Swift had previously held sole rights.

In January 1902, Swift signed an agreement in which the company received the land where its packing operations were to be built, in addition to stock and bonds from the Fort Worth Stock Yards Company. Swift agreed to allow all livestock that it processed to pass through the Fort Worth Stock Yards first. Construction began in February, and in March 1902 the cornerstone for the Swift and Company Office Building was laid. Armour's first buildings were built about the same time, and a wide stairway flanked by both Swift and Armour logos led from the east end of Exchange Avenue up the short hill to the packing plants.

Swift and Company engineers designed the two-and-one-half-story brick office building which was erected by contractor John Newsom. As originally built, the most striking feature of the building was the two-story wooden porch that wrapped around three sides of the building, supported by simple Tuscan columns. The interior of the office building was strictly functional with plastered walls and the same mushroom columns used in the packing plant buildings.

The packing-plant operations proved a boon to the local economy, and spurred unprecedented growth in North Fort Worth (the town was separately incorporated in 1902 but annexed by Fort Worth in 1909) and the area prospered. Large centralized meat-packing operations became obsolete during the 1950s, however, and both Armour and Swift began to scale down their operations. Swift closed its plant on May 1, 1971 (Armour had closed in 1962), bringing the era of Fort Worth's giant packing plants to a close.

The property stood vacant for several years, and many of the packing plant buildings were either partially or completely demolished. In 1976, the Swift and Company Office Building was renovated for use as an Old Spaghetti Warehouse restaurant. The leaded glass windows, colorful paint job, rear addition, and exuberant interior decoration date from this rehabilitation. Nonetheless, the building is the most complete and important structure remaining in the Swift and Company complex. It contributes to the Fort Worth Stockyards National Register Historic District established in 1976. ✿

SWIFT & COMPANY OFFICE BUILDING AND STAIRWAY AT THE END OF EXCHANGE AVENUE

A commanding three-story brick building, the Thannisch Block is located on the northeast corner of Main Street and Exchange Avenue – the crossroads of the Fort Worth stockyards area's commercial district. After Armour and Swift located their packing plant operations here in 1902, many developers saw the need for businesses that catered to cattlemen as well as to stockyards and packing plant employees. One of those was Colonel Thomas Marion Thannisch (1853-1935) who came to North Fort Worth early in 1902 and opened the Stock Yards Inn Bar.

Thannisch entered the hotel business in 1904 when he bought land at the corner of Main and Exchange and constructed the Stock Yards Club Saloon, a wood-frame structure with furnished rooms above and a bar below. He hoped that a new streetcar line, which was to terminate at his building, would enhance his business opportunities. In June 1906 Thannisch purchased two additional lots to the east of the Stock Yards Club Saloon and hired contractor C. E. Brown to build the first portion of the Thannisch Block building. It housed retail establishments including a bar, contractor, and physician's offices on the first floor and hotel rooms on the second and third floors.

By 1913, Thannisch was able to demolish the old Stock Yards Club Saloon and hire the local architectural firm of Field and Clarkson (E. Stanley Field and Wiley G. Clarkson) to enlarge the Thannisch Block. Well integrated with the original structure, the new addition made Thannisch's eighty-six room hotel and retail facility the most prominent commercial building in the area. Robert L. Chandler, a restaurant and hotel manager, ran the operation, which was called the Hotel Chandler. True to Thannisch's expectations,

it was a familiar stopping place for those who came to the stockyards on business as well as for those who lived and worked in the area.

The retail tenants changed over the years, as did the name of the hotel. In 1924, it was called the Planters Hotel; from 1925-1949 it was the Stock Yards Hotel; and from 1950 to 1981 the facility was called the Right Hotel. By the time it was closed by the Fort Worth Public Health Department in 1981 for numerous code violations, the Right Hotel had clearly become the wrong place to be. Thannisch's heirs sold the property to Tom Yater and Marshall Young in 1982 with the understanding that it would be rehabilitated.

The men decided to restore the building's exterior and adapt the interior for use as a small, exclusive hotel. Ward Bogard of Ward Bogard and Associates was the project architect, and Kay Howard of Austin designed the interiors, which follow several frontier themes. The interior of the Thannisch Block was completely reconfigured, and the building now houses the fifty-two-room Stockyards Hotel, which opened in 1984, as well as restaurant, bar, and retail space. The Thannisch Block contributes to the Fort Worth Stockyards National Register Historic District established in 1976 and was designated as a Recorded Texas Historic Landmark in 1984. ⊛

THANNISCH BLOCK

THANNISCH BLOCK DETAIL

*F*ort Worth has been "Cowtown" for much of its existence, and many events related to the cattle industry have become traditions here. The first "fat stock show" was held in 1896 under a stand of trees near the stockyards and moved to a number of temporary North Side locations over the next few years. With the establishment of the Armour and Swift packing plants in 1902 and the resulting increase in the regional market, interest in an annual livestock exhibit grew. Stock show promoters approached the Fort Worth Stock Yards Company, Armour, and Swift to secure funding for the construction of a hall that would provide a permanent home for a show to be called the National Feeders' and Breeders' Show.

Chicago architect Berkley Brandt designed this concrete-stuccoed brick arena, which was constructed by the Texas Building Company just west of the Livestock Exchange Building. The two structures form the architectural anchor for the stockyards area. The Coliseum was completed in February 1908, and the official public opening was held on March 11, 1908. Cost of the 12,000-seat arena was approximately $200,000.

The imposing Mission-style building has an elegant yet utilitarian design, focused on the arena roof which is supported by steel trusses instead of view-obscuring columns. Enormous arched windows and a skylight in the center of the roof provide ample light, although the Coliseum did have electricity when it was first built. Two office pavilions with red tile roofs project from the main arena, flanking eight sets of double-entry doors.

Built as a stock show exposition hall, the Coliseum hosted the National Feeders' and Breeders' Show from 1908 until 1917 and the Southwestern Exposition and Fat Stock Show from 1918 until 1942, after which time the event was moved to Will Rogers Coliseum. In 1918, the Coliseum was the site of the world's first indoor rodeo. It has also been the site of numerous other community events, including performances by Enrico Caruso, Elvis Presley, Harry James, and many other noted musicians and bands. Diaghileff's Ballet Russe performed here in 1916, and evangelist Billy Sunday preached a revival in the Coliseum from November 1918 to January 1919. Truly a focal point for community life, the facility was also used for school sporting events and graduations as well as professional boxing, wrestling, and roller derby.

The City of Fort Worth purchased the Coliseum from the Fort Worth Stock Yards Company in 1936 and, despite attempts to sell the building in the 1940s, still owns it today. Following a difficult period in 1983-1984 when preservationists sought to have the deteriorating building designated as an historic structure – a measure opposed by the city leaders who feared it would impede development plans – the City of Fort Worth undertook a $3 million restoration of the facility in 1985-1986. Ward Bogard was the preservation architect, and Freese and Nichols were the project engineers. The project uncovered and repaired the original skylight and windows, replastered the stucco exterior, repainted the windows and trim in the original adobe red color, and added much-needed heating and air conditioning systems. The Coliseum contributes to the 1976 Fort Worth Stockyards National Register Historic District. It was designated as a State Archaeological Landmark in 1984 and as a City of Fort Worth Landmark in 1983. ⊛

THE COLISEUM

THE COLISEUM

53

TALBOTT-WALL HOUSE

$\mathcal{N}$ew houses continued to be built on Samuels Avenue after the Armour and Swift packing plants opened, despite the fact that the proximity of the slaughterhouses gave the air a distinct tinge. Dr. Richard D. Talbott (c. 1860-1937), one of Tarrant County's pioneer physicians, was born in Ohio and attended medical school in Tennessee before coming west to seek his fortune. Family accounts say that Talbott had no destination in mind when he boarded a west-bound train in 1884, but he got off in Handley where he practiced medicine for five years before moving his office to Birdville. Talbott married Elizabeth Holman of Birdville, and in 1898 the couple bought this property on Samuels Avenue. For several years the Talbotts lived in a cottage that had been erected by previous owners but, in 1903, they tore down the cottage and built this house.

Dr. Talbott died in 1937, but Elizabeth Talbott continued to live here until her own death in 1945. Frances Talbott Wall, the couple's only child, inherited the house and lived here with her husband, Lewis D. Wall, Sr., who worked in investments and real estate. The Walls were a long-time Samuels Avenue family. Charlotte and B. S. Wall, Lewis Wall's grandparents, built their own house just down the street at 748 Samuels Avenue. The Talbott-Wall House remained in the Wall family until 1990, a few years after Frances Wall's death in 1987.

The charming Dutch Colonial Revival house sits on a large tree-covered lot on the west side of Samuels Avenue. Decidedly eclectic in its design, the house has the hallmark gambrel roof, dormer-like upstairs porches, and Corinthian columns supporting the front porch as well as shingles covering the second story. Early Dutch Colonial Revival houses are rare in Fort Worth, and this is the city's most interesting example of the style. ⊛

*A*fter the Armour and Swift companies established their meatpacking operations, they also became involved in related real estate, transportation, and publishing ventures. Among the companies they established was the North Fort Worth Townsite Company, which focused its primary development efforts in Diamond Hill north of the stockyards area. The company also built houses in other North Side neighborhoods, including this Shingle-style residence, which sits at an angle to the street on its bluff-top Grand Avenue site.

The first person to live in the house was Clarence E. Lee, editor of the *Fort Worth Live Stock Reporter* and secretary-treasurer of the firm that published the *Reporter*, the Reporter Publishing Company. Not surprisingly, the Reporter Publishing Company was owned by Armour and Swift. Lee lived here for about five years but only owned the house for one day – when he was the middleman in a real estate deal involving the North Fort Worth Townsite Company, J. M. Abbott, and T. H. Marberry.

After Lee moved out, the house had a number of tenants until it was purchased in 1922 by Sammie and Fred S. Gorczyca. Mr. Gorczyca was a clerk at Swift and Company. Many immigrants from central and eastern Europe came to Fort Worth to work in the stockyards during its first years of operation—the Gorczyca family arrived in 1905. These families put down community roots, and today a number of North Side institutions (see St. Demetrios Greek Orthodox Church) still reflect the ethnic heritage of stockyards workers. Sammie Gorczyca lived in this house until her death in 1978 at the age of ninety-three. Family members sold the house that same year, and it has had a number of owners since.

Although a late example of the Shingle style, this house is the best instance of this uniquely American form remaining in Fort Worth. The style was not common here, and this example is striking not only for its design but also for the way the structure is set at an angle to relate both to Grand Avenue, on which it fronts, and Sixteenth Street, which dead-ends into Grand just east of the house. All parts – including the porch columns – of the one-and-one-half-story bungalow are covered with unpainted shingles. The rounded balcony-tower centered between the two front dormers is typical of the Shingle style, but the railing is a relatively recent addition. This house contributes to the Grand Avenue National Register Historic District, which was listed in the National Register of Historic Places in 1990. ❀

LEE-GORCZYCA HOUSE

*I*n 1916 there were about 2,000 Greeks living in Fort Worth, mostly immigrants from Greece and Turkey. Many were packing house workers, but some had saved their wages and purchased farms or established small businesses. Although a few Greeks came to Fort Worth during the 1890s – the first was Demetreos Anagnostakis who arrived in 1892 – the largest numbers came after the Armour and Swift packing plants were established in 1902. Most lived in North Fort Worth, in the area that is now known as the North Side. In 1910 a group of five men met to organize St. Demetrios Hellenic Orthodox Church, today called St. Demetrios Greek Orthodox Church. It was reputedly the first Greek Orthodox parish in Texas and the Southwest. The first services were held in rented quarters in downtown Fort Worth, but increasing numbers led the congregation to purchase land on the North Side in December 1916 and construct this building the following year.

Local architect Ludwig B. Weinman designed the brick church in a vaguely Byzantine style with a tiled cross-gable roof and high semi-circular parapets on the west, north, and south elevations. The front parapet has a cast-stone panel with the name of the church – The St. Demetrios – in Greek, and the cornerstone is inscribed both in Greek ("I have been set as a foundation stone in the year of our savior in February 1917") and English ("Hellenic Orthodox Church erected in February 1917"). Unique in Fort Worth, this building vividly evokes the rich cultural heritage brought to Fort Worth during the first decades of the twentieth century.

The church building and an adjacent church hall, erected in 1940, were the center for activities in the Greek community for many years. During the 1920s after-school Greek classes were held for school children, and through the years a number of Greek fraternal organizations met at the church. A bread and pastry sale begun during the early 1960s became a successful fund-raising tool for the congregation, and it has grown today into an annual Greek Food Festival held each November.

Today, the congregation is relatively small in numbers but active in local affairs. They have preserved this important building as well as the legacy of the Greek community in Fort Worth. ◉

ST. DEMETRIOS GREEK ORTHODOX CHURCH – CORNERSTONE

ST. DEMETRIOS GREEK ORTHODOX CHURCH

NORTH SIDE POLICE STATION

*A*fter the City of Fort Worth annexed North Fort Worth in 1909, it also took over responsibility for municipal services such as police, fire, and water. By 1910, the city had a temporary police sub-station located across the street from this building at 1529 North Main Street. The facility must not have been adequate, however, because the city purchased the lot on which this building now stands from the Fort Worth Independent School District in April 1911. The lot was on the northern corner of a larger tract on which the district had constructed the North Fort Worth Public School, later known as Merida G. Ellis School, in 1905.

Sanguinet and Staats designed the station which was constructed by T. J. Clardy & Sons, contractors. The same architects and contractors also planned and built a South Side police station as part of this project. Completed in October 1911, the tiny civic building is a handsomely-scaled orange-red brick structure with a central entry door on each facade. All window and door openings on the ground floor are arched and have limestone voussoirs (the wedge-shaped stones forming the arch) and keystones. The keystone above the Main Street entry has a finely-carved garland–and–shield motif. The second floor, above a limestone belt course and row of brick dentils, is much simpler with rectangular window openings and carved wooden brackets under the eaves.

When it opened, the building housed both police and city waterworks substations. The second floor was partitioned to make sleeping quarters for the police officers. Between 1916 and 1932, city directories also show the building as the location of the North Fort Worth City Hall, perhaps operating as a satellite facility for Fort Worth's main municipal offices downtown. From 1920 until about 1941, the library board operated a branch library on the second floor of the building, renting the space from the City of Fort Worth for $50 per month. During the late 1930s, the Tarrant County Relief Board had a branch office here, and through the 1940s the Texas Department of Public Safety was also located here.

The city sold the building to the Lions Club for $10,000 in 1952, ending over forty years of municipal ownership. The Lions owned the building for eighteen years, and it has had a number of owners and a variety of uses since. ❁

THISTLE HILL

*N*o home in Fort Worth evokes the city's "Cowtown" heritage as does Thistle Hill. Although the house was constructed in 1903, just after the Armour and Swift meat-packing plants opened, its legacy is rooted in the cattle drives that followed the Civil War and in the subsequent establishment of the state's large cattle ranches. Electra Waggoner Wharton, daughter of wealthy pioneer cattleman W. T. Waggoner (see W. T. Waggoner Building), grew up in the family's mansion in Decatur, Texas, where she learned to ride and shoot and was very close to her rancher father. Legend says that Waggoner had Thistle Hill built as a "honeymoon cottage" for his daughter upon her June 1902 marriage to Philadelphia socialite Albert Buckman Wharton, Jr. In fact, plans for the house were not announced until that December – after the Whartons had returned from their honeymoon – but it is quite likely that Electra's father had some role in facilitating the construction of the eighteen-room mansion.

Sanguinet and Staats designed the Colonial Revival house which was built south and slightly west of downtown Fort Worth in an area known as Quality Hill. The two-story red brick house had tall, fluted wooden columns, a wooden balustrade wrapping around the second-floor level of the house, and a green wood-shingled roof with dormer windows and a large central pediment.

The Whartons maintained a lifestyle characterized by fine clothes, automobiles (Wharton owned the city's first dealership), and lavish parties. They lived here from 1904 until 1910 when Waggoner gave each of his children extensive sections of land as well as cattle and horses as a Christmas present. At that point, the Whartons sold the house and moved to their new ranch land located near Vernon.

Thistle Hill was purchased in 1911 by Elizabeth and Winfield Scott for $90,000. Scott had made his initial fortune in ranching, but he also had substantial Fort Worth real estate holdings. The Scotts began an extensive remodeling project, hiring architects Sanguinet and Staats to coordinate it. The home's Colonial Revival detailing was removed, and more formal Georgian-style elements substituted. Massive limestone columns replaced the wooden ones, the balustrade was removed and replaced by a small wrought iron balcony above the main entrance, the roof dormers were removed and the pediment reconfigured, and the wooden shingles were replaced with green glazed tile.

Inside, the house has a large foyer opening onto a dramatic horseshoe-shaped staircase. Public rooms – the library, drawing room, dining room, and billiard room – open off this central hall, and a morning room, kitchen, and tiled porch make up the back of the house. Fine oak woodwork, decorative stenciling, and an aluminum-leaf-on-canvas wall treatment distinguish the decorative elements. Bedrooms, dressing rooms, and bathrooms are located upstairs.

Unfortunately, Winfield Scott died before he moved into the house. Elizabeth Scott and her son, Winfield Scott, Jr., did occupy the house once the remodeling was completed. Mrs. Scott lived a more serene lifestyle than did Electra Wharton, but she was active in social and civic affairs. After her death in 1938, the future of the house became more tenuous. Winfield Jr. had none of his father's industrious work habits – but rather had expensive tastes and sold off much of the house's furnishings. By 1940 he had spent the family fortune and decided to sell his mother's home. It was purchased for $17,500 by the Girls Service League, an organization which provided housing for young women.

The league occupied the house from 1940 until 1968, when major structural problems and the need for modernization prompted the decision to move. Although the Girls Service League had made changes to the structure and had minimal funds for major maintenance projects, the organization's presence preserved the mansion at a time when many of its neighbors along Summit and Pennsylvania avenues were falling to the wrecking ball.

The house was located in what had become a developing medical district, and Fort Worth citizens slowly became aware that one of the last surviving cattle baron mansions was endangered. After an initial survey of the historic buildings conducted by the Junior League of Fort Worth identified the Wharton-Scott House as a site worthy of preservation and the demolition of the historic Robert McCart home galvanized a small group of preservationists, the Save-the-Scott-Home effort began. Numerous fund-raising efforts were undertaken, and slowly the group began to accumulate the monies needed to purchase the house. Despite many setbacks, the group finally concluded a contract with the Girls Service League and received the keys to the mansion in August 1976.

In the years that followed, the organization, renamed Texas Heritage, Inc., began restoration efforts. They resurrected Electra Wharton's original name for the house – Thistle Hill – and began to rehabilitate the roof, plumbing, and electrical systems. Extensive changes ordered by the Scotts made it impossible to restore the house to its original 1903 appearance, so the decision was to return it to its 1912 look. After almost a decade of expensive behind-the-scenes work, restoration of the decorative elements began in the mid-1980s. KVG Architects of Fort Worth has coordinated the preservation plan.

In 1987, the house was chosen as the Historic Preservation Council's Designer Showhouse. Rather than giving free rein to their own artistic ideas, the designers worked with appropriate period paint schemes, wall treatments, and furnishings. The restoration of the mansion and its grounds is an ongoing project of which Fort Worth can be justifiably proud. Thistle Hill is open for tours and may be rented for weddings, receptions, and other events. The mansion was listed in the National Register of Historic Places in 1975. It was designated as a Recorded Texas Historic Landmark in 1977 and as a City of Fort Worth Landmark – it was the first building to receive local designation – in 1976. ⊛

THISTLE HILL

65

THISTLE HILL

*T*he Missouri Avenue Methodist Church, founded about 1889, was first located on the southeast corner of Missouri Avenue and Annie Street in an old schoolhouse and then in an 1895 building which was destroyed by fire. Area residents had attended First Methodist Church downtown before Missouri Avenue Methodist Church was established, but the rapidly developing residential districts just south of the central business district made neighborhood churches practical. The church purchased three lots on the northwest corner of Missouri Avenue and Annie Street, catercorner from the old site, in 1904 and selected architect James E. Flanders (1849-1928) to design this building for them. Flanders, who was Dallas' first architect, came to the city in 1875. He designed the 1903 Trinity Methodist Church in Dallas, which is similar to the Missouri Avenue building, as well as courthouses for Shackelford and Stephens counties.

The asymmetrical yellow-brick church has a sandstone base and a steeply-pitched hipped roof. Square towers–the main belfry tower is taller–with pyramidal pressed-metal roofs flank the curving entrance portico. The eclectic design draws inspiration from the intricate ornamental detailing of architect Louis Sullivan in the terra cotta frieze bands and from the forms of the Prairie School in the extreme roof overhangs and general massing of the building. Fine stained glass windows, both Gothic-arched and rectangular, further enliven the facade. A three-story rectangular education building was built on the west side of the church about 1915.

Inside, the sanctuary originally followed the Akron plan, a design developed in the United States in response to the Protestant Revivals of the post-Civil War era and named for the Ohio city where it was first used. The layout places the pulpit in one corner of the sanctuary with the pews arranged in arched rows on a floor that slants towards the pulpit. A room to the side of the main sanctuary was separated from it by means of a moveable wall which could be raised or lowered depending on the number of people attending the service. The Akron plan layout was altered when the church was remodeled in 1950. First Christian Church in downtown Fort Worth, built in 1914-1915, still utilizes the Akron plan.

In 1950 the Missouri Avenue Methodist congregation voted to sell the church to St. Andrew's Methodist Church, an African-American congregation. Founded as a mission in 1888, the church had previously been located on East Rosedale. St. Andrew's undertook a remodeling project, changing the sanctuary to a more conventional arrangement and taking out the moveable wall, and held their first services here on May 20, 1951. St. Andrew's joined the Central Texas Conference of the United Methodist Church in 1970 and became St. Andrew's United Methodist Church. The congregation continues to preserve and worship in this delightful and unusual building. ⊛

MISSOURI AVENUE METHODIST CHURCH/ST. ANDREWS UNITED METHODIST CHURCH

FLATIRON BUILDING

*A*cknowledged as the earliest remaining skyscraper in Fort Worth, the Flatiron Building is important as an example of high-rise design outside Chicago and the major East Coast cities. It is the only true flatiron building in Texas. Although its seven stories are today dwarfed by even the most pedestrian office towers, the Flatiron is one of the most recognized historic buildings in the city – sharing that honor with the Tarrant County Courthouse and Thistle Hill. Designed by local architects Sanguinet and Staats and built by the firm of Buchanan and Gilder for $70,893, the building is an important regional interpretation of the principles of the Chicago School in which architects used steel-frame construction to support tall buildings and designed structures to emphasize their verticality. It also follows architect Louis Sullivan's three-part formula for high-rise buildings with its two-story base, simple shaft or mid-section, and top-floor capital.

The building is located on an odd, triangle-shaped lot at the intersection of Houston and Ninth streets and Jennings Avenue. Dr. Bacon Saunders (1855-1925), a surgeon who was also dean of the Fort Worth Medical College, bought the lot in 1906 and reportedly decided on the triangular form for the building after seeing the 1902 Flatiron Building in New York City designed by Daniel H. Burnham. Sanguinet and Staats originally designed a ten-story building, but a poor economic climate in 1907 led Saunders to build only a seven-story structure. Saunders had his medical offices and laboratory on the top floor of the building, and a drug store occupied the ground floor. Many of the other early tenants were also physicians.

The steel-framed structure is clad in a buff-colored brick with limestone trim. Steel-frame construction allowed for a relatively unobstructed floor plan in which office space could be flexibly divided. The floors are not large, however, and contain about 2,500 square feet of rentable space each. Large plate-glass windows provide both good natural light and efficient cross ventilation. The building has an elevator – a practical necessity for any high-rise structure – with a beautifully ornate iron cage, and marble wainscoting in the main lobby.

Outside, the main entrance and the second and seventh floors have a distinctive geometric ornamentation that is reminiscent of Sullivan's work. A belt course, or continuous band, around the building above the second floor features carved lion or panther heads. Before the railroad arrived in 1876, a Dallas newspaper charged that Fort Worth was such a sleepy little town that a panther could sleep undisturbed in its streets. Local residents saw the reference to the panther as a compliment – perhaps because they liked the cat's spirit and temperament – and Fort Worth adopted the nickname of "Panther City." Several buildings in Fort Worth have used panther or cattle motifs (see United States Post Office and Will Rogers Coliseum) to give the buildings a regional identity.

The building has passed through a number of owners in recent years and has been vacant since the late 1970s. Various adaptive reuse plans have been proposed, including downtown housing, and the building still receives strong community interest and support. The Flatiron Building was listed in the National Register of Historic Places in 1971. It was designated as a Recorded Texas Historic Landmark in 1970 and as a City of Fort Worth Landmark in 1994. ❀

FLATIRON BUILDING

FLATIRON BUILDING

*A*mong Fort Worth's historic churches, Allen Chapel African Methodist Episcopal is particularly significant because it houses one of the community's oldest African-American congregations and because its handsome Gothic Revival building was designed by noted African-American architect William Sidney Pittman (1875-1958). The church was founded in 1870 by a circuit-riding minister known only as Reverend Moody and five local individuals, as the African Methodist Episcopal Church. In 1878, the church bought the land on which this building now stands and shortly thereafter changed the named of the church to Allen's Chapel AME Church (the apostrophe and "s" were dropped in 1898) in honor of Richard Allen (1760-1831), an African-American Philadelphia minister who was the first bishop of the African Methodist Episcopal church.

The property, located six blocks from the Tarrant County Courthouse on the northeastern edge of the central business district, was prominently located in a growing African-American neighborhood. After the arrival of a new minister, Rev. S. R. Jenkins, in 1912, the church decided to raze its 1887 building and construct a larger, more modern facility on the site. Pittman, the son-in-law of Booker T. Washington, was selected as the architect for the project. He was a graduate of Tuskeegee Institute and the Drexel Institute of Art, Science and Industry in Philadelphia and had practiced architecture since 1904. Few of his documented buildings are still standing, but his known projects include the 1907 "Negro Building" at the Jamestown Exposition, the Twelfth Street YMCA in Washington, D. C., and the 1916 Knights of Pythias Hall (now Union Bankers Life) and St. James AME Church in Dallas. Pittman moved to Dallas in 1913, so it is likely that he was able personally to supervise the Allen Chapel project.

Money for construction costs was raised from the congregation. Over 100 members contributed $25 of their Christmas savings in December 1912 to begin the construction fund, and work on the building started shortly thereafter. The names of these members are listed on a white marble slab in the vestibule. William Reed and Sons of Fort Worth built the building. Work was done as money was raised, and the $20,000 structure was dedicated on July 22, 1914.

The Gothic Revival building is constructed of buff-yellow brick with white sandstone trim. Large stained glass windows depicting Moses holding the ten commandments and Jesus as the good shepherd and a number of smaller windows enliven the facade. The interior design of the church is somewhat unusual. The front of the church faces east, but the chancel faces west. As worshipers enter the church, they pass the pulpit and enter the sanctuary facing the congregation– the opposite of most church plans. Reverend Jenkins, the pastor, reportedly suggested this layout so that congregants would not have to turn to look as other worshipers entered the building. The church interior, including the oak wainscot, pressed metal ceilings, Estey pipe organ, and Gothic-style light fixtures, is well preserved. A handsome interior balcony, wrapping three-quarters of the way around the sanctuary, features stained oak woodwork and seating. The church basement houses a dining room and kitchen which were used during the early years for vocational training classes for maids and butlers. At that time, the church also ran a day nursery for the children of working parents.

Church members have been very supportive of their historic building. A renovation project undertaken in 1982-1983 has helped to preserve many of the church's original features. Allen Chapel was listed in the National Register of Historic Places in 1984 and designated as a Recorded Texas Historic Landmark in 1983. ⊕

ALLEN CHAPEL AFRICAN METHODIST EPISCOPAL CHURCH

ALLEN CHAPEL AFRICAN METHODIST EPISCOPAL CHURCH

*L*ocal carpenter and contractor Charles W. Maxwell (d. 1912) built his South Side home in 1904, about the time that Fort Worth's residential development began to push southward out of the central business district. Maxwell signed the chimney, giving his name as the builder of the house. He and his wife Katie lived here until 1907 when they sold the house to James Liston, Sr. (c. 1852-1917).

Liston was a saloonkeeper who owned two bars on Jones and Calhoun streets, in the part of Fort Worth known as Hell's Half Acre. Although the Acre was not the wild and wooly place that it had been during the 1870s and 1880s, there was still enough business from railroad travelers and thirsty citizens for Liston to make a reasonable living. Liston was shot and killed in a late-night robbery on his back porch in 1917 – newspaper accounts indicated that he had brought the day's receipts home with him. His widow Delia continued to live here until her death in 1939. The house remained in the Liston family until 1952 when the estate of Marie Liston, widow of James Liston, Jr., was settled and the house was sold to Sallie Harris. Mrs. Harris lived here until 1972. Since that time, the house has had a number of owners, including Glenda and Ronald Sheffield who rehabilitated the structure in the early 1980s.

The Maxwell-Liston House is a late example of a turreted Queen Anne-style house, rare in Fort Worth (see the Garvey-Veihl House, the other major example). The full porch, supported by ten fluted Ionic columns, wraps around three sides of the structure, but the open tower or turret with a bell-shaped roof above the northeast corner of the porch is the most striking aspect of the home's design. Other decorative elements include the carved wooden panels in the front gables and an oval attic window. This form of the Queen Anne style, which uses classical columns rather than spindlework on the porch and has more restrained decorative detailing, is a later development of the style. It is a transition between Victorian design and early asymmetrical Colonial Revival houses which drew loosely on the decorative detailing of Colonial Georgian and Adam-style houses.

Despite the chain-link fence surrounding the property, the Maxwell-Liston House has an imposing presence in this small South Side neighborhood. The house was designated as a Recorded Texas Historic Landmark in 1985. ⊛

MAXWELL-LISTON HOUSE

MAXWELL-LISTON HOUSE

REEVES-WALKER HOUSE

$\mathcal{H}$emphill Street, a long north-south boulevard, begins just south of downtown Fort Worth. During its heyday in the teens and twenties, it was a solid residential street lined with large bungalows, four-squares, and other residences of eclectic design. The street is now largely commercial in character, and many of the houses have either been demolished or insensitively altered for use as business sites or multi-family dwellings. One of the best preserved survivors is the Reeves-Walker House, built about 1907-1908 for Mattie and William Reeves (1858-1941). Reeves operated William Reeves & Company, a private banking firm. He also had interests in several other Texas banks, including First State Bank and Trust Company of Fort Worth which he organized in 1908. Reeves served as president of the bank for three years but then dissolved it to concentrate on his private banking and brokerage business. He purchased the block on which this house stands in January 1907 and presumably began construction of the house shortly thereafter.

The new house was a large two-and-one-half story structure, a classically-detailed Queen Anne design, which was a mixture of complex Victorian form and Colonial Revival detailing. It is clad in yellow-buff brick with cast stone trim – including quoins – now painted dark red. There is a circular portico with a broad, flairing stairway at the main entrance as well as front and side porches and a porte-cochere, all supported by clustered floral-capped columns. Tall chimneys, dormers, and intersecting gables contribute to the Victorian feel of the house. A carriage house, located behind the main structure, uses the same materials as the residence and follows its general design scheme. Inside, the house retains its original dark oak woodwork including a massive staircase, paneling, and fireplace mantels. A 1914 biographical sketch about Reeves described his house as "one of the handsomest homes in Texas."

In 1917, the Reeves sold the house to Myrtle and John L. Walker (c. 1873-1961), owner and president of the Walker Grain Company – a grain brokerage firm. The Walker family occupied the home through the early 1960s, selling it in 1967 to the Ray Crowder Funeral Home. It served as a funeral home under various owners, including former Fort Worth city council member Louis Zapata, until 1987, when lawyer James Stanley purchased it for use as his law office. His wife, Christi Stanley, coordinated the renovation of the house and its conversion to office use. The Reeves-Walker House contributes to the Fairmount/Southside National Register Historic District, which was listed in the National Register of Historic Places in 1990 and to the Fairmount/Southside City of Fort Worth Historical and Cultural Landmark Subdistrict, designated in 1990. The house was also designated as a Recorded Texas Historic Landmark in 1984. ⊛

REEVES-WALKER HOUSE

*A*s the last of the 'academy' boarding schools for girls founded in Texas by the Roman Catholic religious order, The Sisters of St. Mary of Namur, Our Lady of Victory Academy is a South Side landmark sited on a square block bounded by Hemphill Street, Shaw Street, College Avenue, and Woodland Avenue. In 1885, the sisters had founded St. Ignatius Academy, also a boarding school, but by the end of the first decade of the twentieth century, it had become too small to accommodate the demand for Catholic education. The sisters purchased the land in August of 1908 and commissioned plans by Sanguinet and Staats. Ground was broken on March 25, 1909, and on August 5 of that year, the cornerstone was laid.

On September 12, 1910, the sisters proudly welcomed thirty-one boarders and forty-one day pupils, even though the facilities, which they had occupied only three days earlier, were not quite finished. Basic items such as the installation of a cookstove and attachment to electric and water supplies were soon completed. The students attended classes and lived in this imposing red brick Gothic Revival building trimmed in white limestone with a gray slate roof. In addition to fourteen classrooms on the first and second floors and dormitory space in the upper stories, the structure also contained an auditorium, chapel, music rooms, library, and – in the basement – kitchen and dining facilities. The campus was designed to be self-sustaining and even had its own dairy cattle.

Inside, the building was dignified and solid. Stained woodwork, maple and pine flooring, built-in venetian blinds, sliding pocket doors with a pointed Gothic arch motif, hexagonal floor tiles and stenciling on the walls and ceiling of the entry hall were among the decorative details. The ornamentation in the public spaces – the auditorium, chapel, and classrooms – was richer than the bedroom and dormitory spaces which had clean lines but were relatively spartan. The chapel featured stained glass windows donated by some of Fort Worth's leading Catholic families, including the Laneris and the Biccochis.

Our Lady of Victory prospered during the 1940s and early 1950s, expanding to a new elementary school building in 1953. In 1956, the junior college program and novitiate were incorporated into the newly-established University of Dallas. When Nolan High School opened in 1961 on Fort Worth's east side, OLV stopped taking boarders and became exclusively an elementary school.

From that time, the building was used as a residence, retirement home, and infirmary for members of the order. In 1988, the sisters built a new retirement facility on the northwest corner of the block, vacating the main building. Efforts to sell the historic structure were unsuccessful, and in December 1991 the sisters auctioned off the building's furnishings and some of the stained glass windows, venetian blinds, and doors. Demolition seemed imminent when a task force led by the Historic Preservation Council for Tarrant County was formed to market the building and explore alternative uses. Historic Landmarks, Inc., a nonprofit corporation formed to purchase and redevelop this and other historic properties, acquired the building and 2.99 acres of land in May of 1993. The group plans to rehabilitate the structure and use it for offices and community facilities. Our Lady of Victory was designated as a City of Fort Worth Landmark in 1994. ⊛

OUR LADY OF VICTORY

OUR LADY OF VICTORY

OUR LADY OF VICTORY

*S*t. Andrew's Episcopal Church had its beginning with an Episcopal mission church established in Fort Worth in 1873 by Reverend Alexander C. Garrett, bishop of the Missionary District of North Texas. Garrett traveled widely seeking support for his mission work, and while on a train running between New Haven and Hartford, Connecticut, met John Henry Smith, senior warden of a small parish in Norwalk, Connecticut. Smith invited Garrett to his church to speak about the effort to bring the railroad to Fort Worth and the need for funds for church work in Texas. At the close of the speech, Smith offered Garrett $500 to build a church in Fort Worth, asking that the church be named St. Andrew's. Garrett agreed to his request.

The wooden church was erected in 1877 at the corner of East Fifth and Commerce (Rusk) streets, where it served the congregation until this building was constructed. Designed by Sanguinet and Staats, the Gothic Revival building is reminiscent of an English medieval parish church. Ground was broken on April 13, 1909, but work was halted after the foundation was completed so that additional funds could be raised to satisfy mortgage requirements. Construction work, handled by William Miller Sons and Company of Pittsburgh, Pennsylvania, was completed and the church formally dedicated on May 12, 1912. Shortly after the 1912 church was completed, the older wood-frame building was moved to Lamar Street, placed beside the newer building, and used as a parish hall. It was demolished in 1949 when the present parish house, designed by Preston M. Geren, architect and engineer, was built.

Built of gray dolomite, a hard limestone from Carthage, Missouri, St. Andrew's is in a cruciform plan, a nave with single side aisles and a single transept (the cross arm of a cruciform church) crossing. There are two corner towers on the west or front facade with entry porticos parallel to the transept. The rose window over the altar was crafted in England; all of the other stained glass windows were made by the Jacoby Art Glass Company of St. Louis. The interior features extensive wood wainscot and paneling, wood rood screen, and exposed wood roof beams and ceiling coffers. The pulpit is from the 1877 wooden church building. St. Andrew's remains a vital force in the community and has a long-standing commitment to the care and preservation of this handsome building. ◈

ST ANDREW'S EPISCOPAL CHURCH

85

ST ANDREW'S EPISCOPAL CHURCH

For many years, this diminutive, five-sided building was tucked behind Fort Worth library buildings (the Carnegie until 1939, then the Fort Worth Public Library from 1939 to 1990). Its owner, William Bryce (1861-1944), purchased the lot in 1909 after a portion had been deeded to the City of Fort Worth for right-of-way purposes. Between the angle forced by the library building and the portion of the lot lost to right-of-way, Bryce had limited options in determining the size and shape of the building he would erect on this oddly-shaped plot. The resulting building is, however, a tiny jewel located just across the street from the site of the building that served as Fort Worth's City Hall during Bryce's years of business and community service.

Bryce, whose Arlington Heights home is also a landmark structure (see Fairview), ran the Bryce Building Company, a brick contracting business, and was involved in many other real estate and development ventures. Between 1911 and 1944 he shared the ground-floor space of his 2,900 square-foot office building with some of these concerns, including the Fairmount Land Company, Trinity Heights Land Company, and the Bryce Land Company. Upstairs space was leased to a variety of tenants through the years including the Order of Aztecs and the Royal Flying Corps, which used the building to house its officers during World War I. When Bryce died in 1944, the building was purchased by his long-time friend and business associate, C. B. Grafa, who continued to operate his real estate office from this location.

In subsequent years, the building housed an architect, insurance offices, an accountant, and several restaurants—including the locally popular Hamburg House. A fire in September 1982 closed the Hamburg House and threatened the survival of the building. Demolition was imminent when Betty and Joseph D. Ambrose purchased the building in 1983. Cauble Hoskins Architects sensitively rehabilitated the tiny structure for the Ambroses, returning it to use as office space. In 1990, when the 1938 Fort Worth Public Library was demolished, the Bryce Building, which had been hidden from view, became much more visible. The building currently houses attorney Jack Strickland's law offices. The Bryce Building was listed in the National Register of Historic Places in 1984 and designated as a Recorded Texas Historic Landmark in 1983. ⊛

BRYCE BUILDING

*H*enry W. Williams, Sr. (1838-1925), a native of Georgia, moved to Sherman in 1873 where he ran a drug store. His wife died in 1880, leaving him with a son, Henry Williams, Jr., who was about eight years old. By 1884 both father and son had relocated to Fort Worth, where the elder Williams opened a wholesale drug business. He also served as vice-president of Farmers and Merchants National Bank. In 1907 Williams bought the property on which this house now stands, part of the failed early 1890s Arlington Heights development. At this time, most of the prime residential development was taking place south of downtown Fort Worth, not to the west. Williams' substantial home was one of the first in this development, but it was followed in only a few years by many others.

Although no records confirming the architect of this house have been located, it is thought to be the work of Sanguinet and Staats, based on stylistic similarities to their other designs of the period The eclectic Neoclassical house has a striking full-height entry porch supported by fluted Corinthian columns with a lower full-width porch which wraps around the sides of the structure. Although the symmetrical facade is blocky, the two-story house possesses a sense of grace in its detailing, including the cast-stone quoins, elaborate lintels with a swag motif, slate roof, arched dormer windows, and leaded glass windows. The exterior brick has been painted, two screened porches enclosed, and the interior of the house remodeled.

Following Henry Williams' death, the house was purchased in 1926 by Olive and John Roby Penn (c. 1876-1958). Penn came to Fort Worth in 1920 after he was selected as president of the Texas Pacific Coal & Oil Company, which was beginning to phase out its coal mining and brick making operations in Thurber and focus on the oil business. He also served on the Fort Worth City Council from 1927 to 1933 and headed the NRA's (National Recovery Act) Fort Worth Compliance Board, which promoted Depression-era job development, during the early years of Franklin Roosevelt's presidency. Olive Penn died in 1947, and John Roby Penn in 1958. Since that time, the house has had a several owners. The Williams-Penn House was designated as a Recorded Texas Historic Landmark in 1982 and as a City of Fort Worth Landmark in 1993. ⊗

WILLIAMS-PENN HOUSE

*A*lthough cattle baron Samuel Burk Burnett (1849-1922) did not build the building that now bears his name, he and his heirs owned it for almost seventy years. The imposing Neoclassical building had a rocky start despite the grandeur of its design. Erected in 1913-1914 by the State National Bank at a cost of $450,000, the building was originally called the State National Bank Building. Before the structure was completed in February 1914, State National merged with Fort Worth National Bank and disappeared.

By the time Samuel Burk Burnett bought the building early in 1915 and renamed it for himself, two other banks had already occupied the ground floor. Burnett, a former trail driver, owner of the famed 6666 Ranch, one of the founders of the Texas and Southwestern Cattle Raisers Association, and the first president of the Southwestern Exposition and Fat Stock Show, was also an astute businessman. He reportedly paid cash for the building and told a local newspaper that no cattle figured in the deal – only money. At Burnett's death in 1922, his estate was valued at $6 million, primarily in land, cattle, and buildings.

Designed by Sanguinet and Staats, the Burk Burnett Building stands midway in age and size between two of the firm's other Fort Worth skyscrapers – the 1907 Flatiron Building and the W. T. Waggoner Building of 1919-1920. Buchanan and Gilder were the contractors for the project. When it opened, the building, located on a prominent Main Street corner, was touted as the tallest and most modern in town. Steel-frame construction and concrete floors made the building "absolutely fireproof," but the Burk Burnett Building also had its own artesian well, a refrigeration plant to provide chilled water to all drinking fountains, a complete power plant with boilers, elevators that ran at a speed of 600 feet per minute, and an observation deck atop the water tank penthouse on the roof.

Although the building has exquisite Neoclassical detailing, its form is pure twentieth-century commercial design. A two-story base, clad in granite and cream-colored terra cotta is topped by a relatively plain eight-story shaft with terra cotta string courses separating the floors The most delightful portion of the building is the exuberantly detailed two-story capital with a bracketed and crested terra cotta cornice. Inside, the lobby and banking hall have marble wainscoting and vaulted ceilings and the office floors have solid oak doors and moldings.

The main entrance was remodeled in 1953 by Preston M. Geren, and much of the original terra cotta and granite was removed. Following a slow decline that paralleled the abandonment of the central business district, the Burk Burnett Building was purchased by Bass Brothers Enterprises in 1974 from the estates of Burnett and his widow, Mary Couts Burnett. Geren and Associates renovated the building in 1980, a project which included the construction of a new elevator tower on the south side of the building. The building entrance, ground floor, and mezzanine were rehabilitated in the spirit of the original structure by Weeter and Associates in 1984. The office tower is leased to a variety of tenants including the Texas-New Mexico Field Office of the National Trust for Historic Preservation. The Burk Burnett Building was listed in the National Register of Historic Places in 1980. ⊛

BURK BURNETT BUILDING

BURK BURNETT BUILDING

93

Mount Gilead Baptist Church, the mother church for Fort Worth's African-American Baptist congregations, is located on the east side of the central business district in an historically African-American neighborhood. At one time its neighbors included a fraternal lodge, a variety of African-American-owned businesses, and a thriving residential area. Today, the church is one of the few remaining institutions from that community. Mount Gilead was originally founded in 1875 by Rev. C. A. Augusta with fifteen charter members. By 1912-1913, when this building was built, the church had over 1,000 members, and during the late 1930s membership topped 2,200.

A mechanics lien filed by Mount Gilead in 1912 identifies Sanguinet and Staats as the architects of this fine Neoclassical, temple-form building. Other evidence, a plate of Mount Gilead found in a set of printing plates used by African-American architect Wallace A. Rayfield of Alabama to produce architectural plan books, suggests that Rayfield may have designed the building. It is possible that Sanguinet and Staats acted as supervising architects in the execution of Rayfield's design, but no evidence has been found to clarify the situation. J. W. O'Gwin, a contractor working with B. W. Owens of the G. W. Owens Lumber Company, was the project contractor.

The two-story church has a raised basement and a pedimented entrance portico supported by six massive Tuscan columns. Stained glass windows were added after the original building was completed, many honoring the families who made them possible. The stained glass dome in the sanctuary was installed when the church was first built. When it opened, the church boasted a sanctuary that seated 2,000, a day nursery, sewing room, labor bureau, public baths, gymnasium, roof garden, and swimming pool. During the early years the church also ran a business school and operated a hospital next door to the church. Segregation forced many institutions in the African-American community to offer such services which were otherwise not available to community members.

Although the building has been altered over the years – windows in the front part of the raised basement have been covered with tile, the entrance stairways reconfigured, and the stucco infill painted to contrast with the dark brown brick – the church still retains much of its original character. Mount Gilead must now draw its worshipers from throughout the city – a challenge faced by other downtown churches. Nonetheless, it remains an important architectural and institutional community anchor. ⊛

MOUNT GILEAD BAPTIST CHURCH

95

*A*lthough many Craftsman-style houses were built in Fort Worth during the teens and twenties, most were small bungalows. A unique surviving example of a more ambitious Craftsman residence is the clinker brick house constructed by Vila and Julian C. Harris (1885-1977) according to plans drawn by noted designer Gustav Stickley. The plans were first reproduced in the July 1909 issue of Stickley's *Craftsman Magazine* and reprinted in his book *More Craftsman Houses*, published in 1912, which the Harrises owned. Harris, a bookkeeper, was the nephew of Fred Cobb, owner of the Cobb Brick Company. He moved to Fort Worth to work for his uncle shortly after graduating from Dartmouth College.

In October 1912, Harris purchased a large lot in Cobbs Orchard Addition near the brickyard from another relative, William H. Cobb of the W. C. Belcher Land Mortgage Company, and began to build this house. Stickley's design, titled a "Craftsman Stone House with Practical Built-in Fittings," called for a stone exterior, but Harris substituted clinker brick from the Cobb Brick Company. Clinker brick is brick that has become overheated in the kilns and "melted" into twisted glazed forms. Although it was more difficult to lay than conventional brick, clinker brick provided an interesting color and texture – in this case a combination of black and tan. The stone-like forms of clinker brick appealed to those who agreed with Stickley's assertion that beauty could be found in natural materials, simply arranged.

Stickley designed a two-story, rectangular house with a generally symmetrical facade. Massive stone chimneys flank each end of the house and the wide eaves are supported by heavy wooden brackets. Both features are hallmarks of the Craftsman style.

There is a full front terrace, also constructed of clinker brick, and a second-floor wooden balcony, above the main entrance, which opened off a sleeping porch, now enclosed. Although the relatively small, multi-paned wooden casement windows and brick exterior give the house an imposing air, the interior is open, with a warm and informal feeling. Beamed ceilings, fireplaces, and built-in bookshelves and window seats, all typical of Craftsman design, pull the large open spaces together.

This house was one of the first built in the area, and for several years its address in the city directories was simply "Oakland Stop, Cleburne Interurban." Sited on a one-and-one-half acre lot, the house is now surrounded by smaller homes built during the 1920s and 1930s. Complete with its original furnishings, the house remained in the Harris family until 1985. It was designated as a City of Fort Worth Landmark in 1989. ⊛

HARRIS HOUSE

97

*I*n 1855, only two years after the United States Army abandoned Fort Worth leaving the military facility in the hands of civilians, a circuit-riding Disciples of Christ minister, Reverend A. M. Dean, arrived to establish the congregation that would become First Christian Church. Initially, the worshipers met in the log home of Dr. and Mrs. Carroll M. Peak, Fort Worth's first physician and his wife, but moved through a succession of church buildings as the congregation grew.

In 1877, First Christian bought the property on which this building now stands for $1,500 and, in 1878, erected a building that came to be called the Old Rock Church. Though the building was substantial, by 1910 the church had 3,000 members–making it the third largest Disciples of Christ congregation in the world–and church leaders began to think about erecting a larger structure. In 1912, Reverend L. D. Anderson became pastor and, with the support of influential church members such as cattleman Samuel Burk Burnett and banker Major K. M. Van Zandt, the congregation retained the firm of Van Slyke and Woodruff (E. W. Van Slyke and Clyde Woodruff) to design the new building. The old church was demolished, and in 1914 construction began on the present church structure, which is located at one of Fort Worth's main central business district intersections.

The Neoclassical cast-stone building, erected by the Oklahoma City firm of Reinhart and Dononvan Company, has a Greek Cross plan with a tower and copper-clad double dome at the crossing. Two massive pedimented porticos, each with six unfluted Corinthian columns, grace the front and south side of the building. Three sets of paired entrance doors, facing Throckmorton Street, are reached by means of a terraced stairway which splits to encircle a landing with a recessed street-level entry behind an arcade. Most of the church's windows are art or stained glass casement windows depicting lilies and the cross. The windows, as well as the church's seating, organ case, and pulpit furniture were all designed by Van Slyke and Woodruff.

Inside, the arrangement of the sanctuary follows the Akron or auditorium plan which was developed to focus the attention of the audience on the preacher's pulpit (see also Missouri Avenue Methodist Church). When First Christian was built, a moveable wall on the side of the sanctuary could be raised to increase the seating capacity by combining the main sanctuary with an adjacent smaller meeting room. The wall is still present, but is no longer moved. A twenty-four foot diameter stained glass dome highlights the sanctuary ceiling. The church organ was the gift of Samuel Burk Burnett. With the exception of the urns on the front portico, which replaced four original light posts, the church exterior is unaltered, and the interior retains much of its historic fabric. First Christian Church was listed in the National Register of Historic Places in 1983. ⊛

FIRST CHRISTIAN CHURCH

FIRST CHRISTIAN CHURCH

FIRST CHRISTIAN CHURCH

*P*olytechnic Heights, now an East Side Fort Worth neighborhood, was a separate community until it was annexed by Fort Worth in 1922.

It was a small community, built around the Manchester Cotton Mill, until 1891 when Polytechnic College (now Texas Wesleyan University) was founded. A streetcar line, established in 1892, brought students to town, but it also made it practical to construct "suburban" residences. Samuel Selkirk Dillow (c. 1866-1931) opened Polytechnic's first retail business, a grocery store, that same year. Polytechnic grew rapidly between 1900 and 1910 as the college expanded its enrollment and constructed several new buildings. Dillow was involved in his community, serving on the school board and as a city commissioner. He was also the president of the First State Bank of Polytechnic and chairman of the board of trustees of Polytechnic Methodist Church.

Dillow's first home in Polytechnic burned in 1910, but he was committed to the community and decided to build this brick house, completing it in 1912. At the time, it was the eastern-most house on the street and was located just east of Dillow's grocery store which burned and was subsequently demolished in 1984. Dillow lived here until his death, and his daughter Audrey occupied the house until her own death in 1981. Miss Dillow graduated from Texas Woman's College (Polytechnic College was renamed Texas Woman's College in 1914 when it restricted enrollment to women and, in 1935, became Texas Wesleyan College when it was again made coeducational) in 1925 and taught home economics, art, reading, social studies, and spelling in Fort Worth schools – primarily at D. McRae Elementary – until 1963.

The dwelling is a two-story Prairie-style residence, faced in an ochre-colored brick mottled with black. A full porch supported by brick piers and Tuscan columns wraps around the north and east sides of the building. Inside, many original features including stained paneling and light fixtures remain. Miss Dillow willed the house to her alma mater in 1979 because of her family's long connection to Texas Wesleyan. Wesleyan rehabilitated the house in 1982 and currently uses it for alumni offices and as a meeting space. The Dillow House was designated as a City of Fort Worth Landmark in 1989. ⊛

*R*eal estate magnate John C. Ryan (1865-1928) left an enduring legacy in Fort Worth in the many residential neighborhoods that he planned and developed. These range from a four-acre tract platted as the Ryan and Bergin Addition before Ryan was twenty-one years of age to well-known neighborhoods such as Morningside and Ryan Place. It was in Ryan Place that John C. Ryan chose to realize his belief in the City Beautiful Movement, which theorized that planned development based on classical architectural styles and reverence for natural beauty would result in urban park-like neighborhoods that had superb aesthetic and functional qualities. Ryan Place was a restricted development – one of the first in the city, but later typical of many Fort Worth developments – with requirements for building materials (no wood frame houses), street landscaping, and ownership (no African-Americans – a restriction later deemed unconstitutional). Terraced lots, tree-lined streets, and massive stone entrance gates all contributed to the exclusive character of the neighborhood.

Ryan chose to build his own home on Elizabeth Boulevard, named for his wife, about three years after development in the Ryan Place neighborhood had begun. He selected the Fort Worth architectural firm of Field and Clarkson (E. Stanley Field and Wiley G. Clarkson) to design the two-story residence, which was constructed by C. M. Butcher. According to an "Agreement for Building with Bond" signed in July 1914, the house was to be completed by December 1 of that year for the sum of $16,283, and a bill dated February 1, 1915 shows a total cost of $19,685.69.

The Italian Renaissance-style house covers two large lots at the corner of Fifth Avenue and Elizabeth Boulevard. Constructed of tan brick with a green ceramic tile roof, the symmetrically-arranged house has a very formal feel. A full porch supported by Tuscan columns shelters three of the seven pairs of French doors spaced across the front of the home. Decorative brackets support the wide, boxed eaves.

In 1918, Elizabeth and John Ryan sold their residence to Mazzie Bewley and Bert K. Smith (c. 1877-1958) and moved to 2530 Ryan Place Drive. Smith was a grain dealer, co-owner of the Smith Brothers Grain Company, who also had interests in other business concerns including serving as vice-president of The Fair Store and the Star Refining and Producing Company and president of the Grain and Cotton Exchange of Fort Worth.

The house remained in the Smith family until 1965, and it has had a number of owners since. Dr. John and Sara Jeffers bought the house in 1977 and, in 1981, allowed it to be used as the Historic Preservation Council for Tarrant County's first Designers Showhouse. At that time the house was rehabilitated in keeping with its historic character, and the kitchen was updated and remodeled. Ownership changed and, in 1994, the home again served as the Designers Showhouse benefitting the Historic Preservation Council. Elizabeth Boulevard was listed in the National Register of Historic Places in 1979 as Fort Worth's first residential historic district and designated as a City of Fort Worth Historic and Cultural Landmark Sub-district in 1980. The Ryan-Smith House contributes to these districts and is a building which has both benefitted from and contributed to historic preservation efforts in Fort Worth.

*W*illiam M. Harrison (1891-1976), at the time a banker, automobile supply dealer, and manager of Star Refining and Producing Company and later founder and president of Crown Machine and Tool Company, bought the Elizabeth Boulevard lot on which this house stands in May 1913. At that time, there were fewer than half-a-dozen houses built on the street, but the area had a good reputation for up-and-coming businessmen. The name of the architect who designed this Prairie-style residence for Harrison is not known, but it was one of the more progressive designs on a street noted primarily for its traditional Period Revival compositions.

This boxy, two-story house is stuccoed and trimmed with red brick. The low-pitched hipped roof, massive square columns supporting the one-story porch, and transomed casement windows are hallmarks of Prairie-style design, while the details – ceramic tiles with red and green geometric designs and the elegant front door with stained glass panels – draw their inspiration from Mission architecture. The porte-cochere and porch above it on the east side of the house (both now enclosed) are later additions, but the form is compatible with the original design.

This is the best surviving Prairie-style house in Fort Worth and is a charming smaller residence among the many large homes on Elizabeth Boulevard.

Harrison and his wife Margaret lived here until 1922, and Emily and O. K. Shannon purchased the home in 1923. Shannon was for many years the president and general manager of Fort Worth Gas Company, and his son, Ogden K. Shannon, Jr., who also lived here for a time with the elder Shannons, was an attorney. The house remained in the Shannon family until 1953, and it has had a number of owners since. It contributes to the Elizabeth Boulevard National Register Historic District, which was listed in the National Register of Historic Places in 1979, and to the City of Fort Worth's Historic and Cultural Landmark Sub-district which was designated in 1980. ◉

HARRISON-SHANNON HOUSE / PORCH DETAIL

*B*LACK GOLD • 1917-1930s

Fort Worth was a major supply center for cattle ranches and towns in West Texas, and this role increased after oil became big business. Oil companies set up their headquarters here, oilmen who drilled the fields between Fort Worth and Midland built homes here, and all types of organizations, businesses, and services were established to assist the growing community. Amon Carter's unceasing promotion of Fort Worth and West Texas through the pages of the Fort Worth Star-Telegram *and his own civic endeavors strengthened the ties that were already in place. There was a growing sense of Fort Worth as a hub city – a place as modern and up-to-date as any other major metropolitan area – and boosters were eager to erect buildings that would reflect that status and sophistication.*

W. T. Waggoner (1852-1934) was drilling shallow water wells on his cattle ranch near Electra in 1903 when he first struck oil. "Damn the oil, I want water!" was Waggoner's reported reaction, but he accepted his fate and, beginning with his first wells drilled in 1911, parlayed the new commodity into a fortune said to be worth in excess of $50 million. Waggoner had a house in Fort Worth in addition to his ranch holdings, and a number of his business operations focused on the prospering cowtown turned oil-town.

Among his investments was the W. T. Waggoner Building – actually owned by his wife Ella Waggoner – an office tower which was home to many oil companies and related businesses. Designed by Sanguinet and Staats and built at a cost of $1.5 million by C. S. Lambie & Company of Denver, Colorado, the twenty-story Chicago-style skyscraper was planned to include every modern office amenity. Stressing that "no feature of the building has been stinted," an early promotional brochure also assured prospective tenants that "no money has been wasted in useless ornamentation." The result was a striking U-shaped, steel-framed brick tower set on a two-story base of polished green granite. The U-shaped plan provided light and ventilation for each office space. A two-story capital featured ornamental stone and terra cotta moldings with classical designs. The building was the tallest in Fort Worth when it was first constructed, but it did not hold that title for long in the building boom of the early twenties.

Inside, the first floor bank and entry lobbies had marble paneling, terrazzo floors, and vaulted ceilings. The original banking hall and mezzanine are still intact. Otis elevators, a built-in vacuum cleaning system, and refrigerated drinking water from an artesian well on the property were also among the building's many amenities. The building remained in the Waggoner family until 1962, and it has had a number of owners since. A 1984-1985 renovation project restored the first two floors of the facade, the banking hall, and the third-floor office spaces. Cauble Hoskins Architects prepared the plans and Haws & Tingle served as the general contractors for this undertaking. The remaining office floors were also gutted and refurbished at this time. The W. T. Waggoner Building was listed in the National Register of Historic Places in 1979. ✿

W. T. WAGGONER BUILDING

W.T. WAGGONER BUILDING

W.T. WAGGONER BUILDING

*F*ort Worth's status as a cattle, railroad, and oil center led to expansive thoughts during the years immediately following World War I. Continued business growth prompted community leaders to assess the need for a new, first-class hotel. A group which included department store merchants William Monnig, Sr., and W. C. Stripling as well as tireless Fort Worth promoter and newspaper publisher Amon G. Carter decided that a new hotel was needed and formed the Citizens Hotel Company to erect the building.

Sanguinet and Staats, who had already made a significant impact on Fort Worth's skyline, were selected to design the new showplace. Mauran, Russell and Crowell, a St. Louis firm with expertise in hotel design, served as associate architects. Westlake Construction Company of St. Louis was the project contractor, as identified in a series of construction photographs. Original plans called for a $2 million project, but interest in a luxury facility was so strong that the Citizens Hotel Company decided to build a more elaborate building at a cost of $4 million. Construction began in January of 1920, and the formal opening was held on December 3, 1921.

While it was being planned and under construction, the hotel was called the Winfield Hotel in honor of Mexican-War hero Winfield Scott. It was thought – incorrectly – that Scott had helped to determine the location for the original Fort Worth. Fearing that the historical reference to Scott might be too obscure for a hotel that was to mark Fort Worth's status in the twentieth-century business world, the Citizens Hotel Company directors decided to change the name of the hotel to The Texas – or, as it came to be known for the first thirty-or-so years of its operation, the Hotel Texas. T. B. Baker, hotel manager, claimed that the hotel – despite its Georgian Revival-inspired architecture – was a Texas establishment. "We have Texas men in charge, and we have striven to give it a Texas atmosphere," said Baker in a *Fort Worth Star-Telegram* interview.

The fifteen-story hotel building recalls Sanguinet and Staats' earlier design for the Burk Burnett Building, with terra cotta ornamentation and elaborate window openings on the base or ground floor and top story and a relatively plain red brick shaft between. A touch of regionalism is found in the wide band or architrave at the top of the base which features cow skulls draped with chaining flowers from the Yucca plant alternating with classical medallions. The overall impression is one of formal elegance, appropriate for a luxury hotel in a town which felt its influence growing beyond regional boundaries.

Through the years, the Hotel Texas had many important guests. It may be best known, however, as the place where President John F. Kennedy spent his last night on November 21, 1963, before the fateful trip to Dallas. President and Mrs. Kennedy spent the night in Room 850, which was specially decorated with western paintings, rather than in one of the larger suites because the Secret Service felt they could better protect the Kennedys in a room with only one door.

Despite the addition of a grand ballroom in 1961 and other changes, the hotel survived relatively intact until the late 1960s. In 1967, Sheraton Corporation leased the building and took over hotel operations. During this period, $6 million was spent to remodel the hotel and construct a 230-room annex to the east of the main building. Sheraton renamed the Hotel Texas the Sheraton-Fort Worth in 1970 and continued to operate it until 1978. In 1979, Woodbine Development Corporation acquired the property and renovated it, replacing all of the original windows on the fourth through fourteenth floors, constructing a double-vaulted entrance canopy, and completely reconstructing the hotel's interior. JPJ Architects, Inc. of Dallas coordinated the renovation, and Singer-Christianson & Company of Los Angeles handled the interior design. HCB Contractors of Dallas was the general contractor. During the 1980s the hotel was operated as a Hyatt Regency, but it became the Radisson Plaza Fort Worth in December 1991. The Hotel Texas was listed in the National Register of Historic Places in 1979 and designated as a Recorded Texas Historic Landmark in 1982. ⊗

HOTEL TEXAS/RADISSON PLAZA HOTEL

114

A stunning anchor for the east end of Elizabeth Boulevard, Fort Worth's oldest residential historic district, this elaborate Mediterranean Revival style house was built for oilman Richard Otto Dulaney (1882-1966). Dulaney made his initial fortune in real estate in Oklahoma but shifted his focus to the oil industry when he founded the Fort Ring Oil and Gas Company in 1916. With fellow Fort Worth oilman Floyd J. Holmes, Dulaney also established the Planet Petroleum Company in 1918, which drilled successful wells in Electra and in Wichita County, Texas, as well as in Duncan, Oklahoma. The pair sold the company three years later for $3 million.

Dulaney moved to Fort Worth from Oklahoma in 1919 with his wife, Stella. The December 23, 1922, *Texas Oil World* newspaper makes note of Dulaney's plans to erect this Elizabeth Boulevard mansion and illustrates plans drawn by the architect, Raphael A. Nicolais (1883-1979). Nicolais came to Fort Worth about 1917 and worked as an architect for the firm of Sanguinet and Staats. By 1919 he was in business for himself, but his tenure in Fort Worth was short. He moved to Los Angeles in 1924 where he also practiced architecture, designing many schools, libraries, and other government buildings. Nicolais' design was erected by the Harry B. Friedman Construction Company in 1923.

After his success in the oil business, Dulaney again ventured into real estate, constructing the Petroleum Building in 1927 and the Sinclair Building in 1930. Dulaney also invested in a Colorado uranium mine in 1949, seeing it as an opportunity if atomic energy ever overtook oil as a power source.

The impressive two-story residence is constructed of cream-colored brick and glazed terra cotta with a green tile roof. The arched, floor-length windows on the front and sides of the house were originally doorways which opened onto the balustraded terrace. At the time of Dulaney's death in 1966, the Elizabeth Boulevard area was no longer the prestigious residential neighborhood it had once been. Owners Dr. Richard and Ruby Jo Halden, who acquired the house in 1967, helped to form the Ryan Place Improvement Association and were instrumental, along with many of their neighbors, in revitalizing the area. Elizabeth Boulevard was listed in the National Register of Historic Places in 1979 as Fort Worth's first residential historic district and designated as a City of Fort Worth Historic and Cultural Landmark Sub-district in 1980. This house contributes to both districts. The interior of the house was renovated in 1983 when the residence served as the Historic Preservation Council's Designer Showhouse. ⊗

DULANEY HOUSE

116

DULANEY HOUSE

117

Cottonseed products dealer Marshall A. Fuller and his wife Lillian bought a large corner lot on Elizabeth Boulevard late in 1922 and commissioned local architect Wiley G. Clarkson to design this Spanish Colonial Revival residence. The style was popular in Texas and the Southwest during the 1920s, drawing its inspiration from the Spanish and Mexican colonial architecture of the seventeenth to early nineteenth centuries and from Bertram Grosvenor Goodhue's designs for the Panama-Pacific Exposition of 1915 which celebrated the rich tradition and detailing of Spanish design.

Clarkson's plans for the asymmetrical two-story, stucco-clad house feature the hallmark red tile roof and an elaborate arched entryway with a low relief carved cornice topped by an arched stained glass window with a wrought iron balcony. An arcaded portico on the southeast corner of the house and a corbelled chimney further enliven the facade.

After 1939, Lillian Fuller leased the house to J. Lee Johnson, Jr., and, in 1941, sold it to Susie and Dudley Hiram Snyder, son of pioneer trail driver D. H. Snyder and a cattleman with ranch land in Mitchell and Howard counties. Mr. Snyder died in 1946, but Susie Snyder lived here until her death in 1962. The current owners, Kenneth and Sherry Pounds, purchased the house in 1978 and renovated it in 1989-1990, joining an existing frame garage and servants quarters constructed in 1930 with a storage building to create a separate stucco-clad entertainment and living area, adding a stucco fence around the rear portion of the lot, installing a swimming pool, and painting all of the stucco pink. Mrs. Pounds coordinated the design work for the alterations to her home. This house contributes to the Elizabeth Boulevard National Register Historic District which was listed in the National Register of Historic Places in 1979 as Fort Worth's first residential historic district as well as to the City of Fort Worth's Historic and Cultural Landmark Sub-district designated in 1980. ⊛

FULLER-SNYDER HOUSE

119

SOUTHSIDE MASONIC LODGE/MAGNOLIA CENTRE

On January 26, 1924, Louis L. Horn, master of the Southside Lodge No. 1114 A.F. & A.M. (Ancient Free and Accepted Masons), and other prominent Masons gathered on Magnolia Avenue to witness the laying of the cornerstone for the Southside Lodge's new building on the corner of Fifth and Magnolia avenues. Established in 1915 with fifty-four Southside Lodge members who met above a grocery store, the Masonic presence in the neighborhood grew quickly as the residential area to the south developed. By the mid-1920s there were almost one thousand members and a strong need for the new lodge building.

The three-story Classical Revival building was designed by local architect and engineer James B. Davies, Sr., with the assistance of W. E. Ketchum. Like many earlier fraternal halls, the building was laid out with retail space on the first floor and lodge meeting rooms on the other two floors and mezzanine levels. Renting out the space on the main floor helped the Lodge underwrite the cost of maintaining the building. Harveson and Cole funeral home occupied the ground floor when the building first opened. The facility was intended to provide meeting space not only for Lodge No. 1114 but for other appendant bodies including the Southside Chapter No. 673, Order of the Eastern Star; Southside Chapter No. 378, Royal Arch Masons; and Southside Commandery No. 83, Knights Templar. Separate facilities were required for each group because rituals were secret, even from the related groups which met in the building. The primary facades on Magnolia and Fifth avenues are similar in design and are faced with buff brick and cast-stone trim. On these faces, the design follows the base, shaft, and capital pattern of a classical column in its tripartite composition – pedestal, pilasters/windows, and entablature. The giant fluted pilasters, which are two stories tall, and the large windows – those on the second floor are topped by a broken pediment with an urn in the center – are the most striking decorative details.

Although Magnolia Avenue flourished as a neighborhood commercial area during the 1920s and 1930s, it fell into decline during the 1960s and 1970s. The Masons sold the building to Lodge No. 251 of the Independent Order of Odd Fellows in 1976 who, in turn, sold it for commercial development in 1983. By that time, there was a growing recognition of Magnolia Avenue's significance as an historic district and of the Southside Lodge's status as one of the most substantial and distinctive buildings along Magnolia. Ray Boothe of Boothe & Associates Architects renovated the building in 1985-1986 for office use, naming the project Magnolia Centre. The building was listed in the National Register of Historic Places in 1985 and designated as a contributor to the Fairmount/Southside National Register Historic District and the City of Fort Worth Historic and Cultural Landmark Sub-district in 1990. ⊛

SOUTHSIDE MASONIC LODGE/MAGNOLIA CENTRE

$\mathcal{E}$stablished in 1909 as Fort Worth's fourth Catholic parish, Saint Mary of the Assumption Church was first housed in a wooden building which was almost completely destroyed by fire on August 31, 1922. Determined to rebuild on the same site, the church selected the Fort Worth firm of Sanguinet, Staats and Hedrick to draw plans for its new home. The architects designed a handsome Romanesque Revival building, with a sanctuary seating 500 worshipers, which was constructed of red brick with cast-stone trim. Rev. Anthony Malloy celebrated the first mass in the new church on July 20, 1924. The bell tower on the northeast corner of the church did not originally house any bells, but Rev. Damian Wewers, an assistant pastor who later served as pastor of the church, located bells initially intended for the Sacred Heart Church in Muenster, Texas, purchased them, and had them installed in the Saint Mary's bell tower in 1956.

The Carrara marble altar and sculptures of Jesus, Joseph, and Mary were rescued when the frame church burned and installed in the new building. A series of stained glass windows by the Bavarian craftsman H. Mueller, donated by families in the congregation and installed beginning in 1928 under the tenure of Rev. Aemilian Schmitt, depict events in the life of Jesus. Schmitt also commissioned interior murals including a panel depicting the assumption or ascension of the Virgin Mary into Heaven.

Saint Mary's continues to serve as a neighborhood parish church, ministering to what has become a primarily Hispanic congregation. The church building was listed in the National Register of Historic Places in 1984 and designated as a Recorded Texas Historic Landmark in 1980. ✪

ST MARY OF THE ASSUMPTION CATHOLIC CHURCH

W. I. and Missouri Matilda Nail Cook (1858-1932) made a comfortable living on their cattle ranch near Albany in Shackelford County, and Mrs. Cook was deeply saddened by her husband's death in 1922. When oil was discovered on the Cook Ranch in 1925, Mrs. Cook found that she had the means to provide a fitting memorial for her husband and for her daughter who had died in childbirth in 1901. Fort Worth was the closest major urban center for many West Texas ranchers, and many had family and financial ties to the city. Mrs. Cook decided to establish a hospital for children and working women, called the W. I. Cook Memorial Hospital, and provided both the land and income from her oil royalties to build the facility. The private thirty-bed hospital also housed the Beall Clinic where Mrs. Cook's family physicians, Frank C. Beall and K. H. Beall, practiced.

Local architect Wiley G. Clarkson drew plans for the building with the assistance of Charles O. Chromaster, one of his designers. Construction, handled by contractor Harry B. Friedman, began early in 1927, and the hospital opened on January 28, 1929. The hospital building is set on a beautifully landscaped, terraced site just west of downtown Fort Worth. Another Clarkson design, the Classical Moderne-style Masonic Temple built in 1930-1932, is located just east of the hospital.

More traditional than its neighbor, Cook Hospital is a handsome Second Renaissance Revival building constructed of Indiana limestone with green terra cotta roof tiles and ornate bronze entry gates. The original building consisted of a three-story main rectangular block with a projecting one-story wing housing staff offices. This wing encircled an open, landscaped courtyard which has since been enclosed. Inside, the hospital had an elegant home-like atmosphere with a reception area furnished with leather couches and chairs, carved Italian chests, and brass candlesticks. The room had Italian travertine walls, walnut ceiling beams, and a brown and white marble floor. The floor in the foyer was decorated with the "Tumbling T" brand from Mrs. Cook's ranch. Despite the comfortable feel of the facility, it had the most up-to-date medical facilities available.

In 1952 the general hospital was converted into a children's hospital and the name changed to W. I. Cook Children's Hospital. The Beall Clinic was closing, a local study showed an urgent need for a children's hospital, and the estate left by cotton merchant, rancher, and oil man Tom B. Owens was made available to the hospital to care for children. The facility expanded in 1957-1958 by building a two-story addition on top of the front wing, which increased the hospital capacity to 100 beds. Cook Children's Hospital specialized in cancer treatment, eye-ear-nose-and-throat care, general surgery, and dental care.

In 1985 Cook Children's Hospital merged with Fort Worth Children's Hospital to form Cook-Fort Worth Children's Medical Center, and a new facility was constructed in Fort Worth's hospital district. Cook sold this building to HealthSouth Rehabilitation Corporation in 1989 for use as a rehabilitation hospital. Working with HealthSouth corporate architects, in 1989-1990 Gresham, Smith and Partners designed a complementary three-story addition to the north of the main building and restored the old hospital. Frymire Company was the general contractor for the project. Both the new construction and the adaptive reuse of the historic hospital building were handled in a sensitive manner, giving new life to a building that had housed one of Fort Worth's most beloved institutions. ⊛

W.I. COOK CHILDREN'S HOSPITAL/HEALTHSOUTH REHABILITATION HOSPITAL

W.I. COOK CHILDREN'S HOSPITAL/HEALTHSOUTH REHABILITATION HOSPITAL

W.I. COOK CHILDREN'S HOSPITAL/HEALTHSOUTH REHABILITATION HOSPITAL

127

*R*ecognizing the need for a centralized facility to care for the widows and children of Texas Masons, the Grand Lodge of Texas began the search for an appropriate site in 1885 and a major fund-raising program the following year. Several cities offered proposals, but none met the specifications outlined by the Board of Directors. It was 1898 before the board accepted an offer from Fort Worth's Lodge #148 to donate a site near Polytechnic Heights, southeast of Fort Worth. The facility opened on October 6, 1899, as the Masonic Widows and Orphans Home, but in 1911 became the Masonic Home and School of Texas when the Home for Aged Masons opened in Arlington. The school's current mission is to provide education and care for "needy children and grandchildren of Masons in Texas."

The school not only provided an academic education for students but taught a variety of vocational skills including farming, printing, cooking, woodworking, bookkeeping, typing, drafting, and sewing. Residents grew their own food, had a cattle and dairy ranch, and did printing for various Masonic organizations as well as for the school. Approximately 150 acres of the original 212-acre site were used for agricultural purposes. By 1913, the Masonic Home offered twelve grades of schooling and operated as an independent school district. The facility grew rapidly, and by the mid-1920s there was a pressing need for additional buildings.

During the early 1920s, Fort Worth architect Wiley G. Clarkson was retained to develop the first master plan for the school and to design several new buildings. Among them was the new Administration Building, which replaced a multi-purpose building erected in 1899. Clarkson sited the Administration Building at the top of the drive leading into the campus and laid out the other structures on a north-south axis from the Administration Building with a grassy common between the two rows of buildings. It was a traditional and classical plan for a campus. Clarkson used the Gothic Revival style, a favored form for religious and academic buildings, for each of the campus buildings he designed here.

Contractor James T. Taylor erected the Administration Building in 1925, according to Clarkson's plans. It is the showplace of the Masonic Home complex. A two-story hall composed of red brick and limestone, the building sits on a raised basement built of rusticated limestone blocks. A short central tower, with a covered entryway reached through a Gothic arch, is the most intricately ornamented portion of the building. Four stepped limestone buttresses and a carved limestone parapet featuring the Masonic emblem flanked by a mixture of finials and trefoil ornaments highlight this central section of the building. Limestone quoins and the beltcourse above the second floor integrate the tower ornamentation with the overall building design. The hardwood front entry doors also have leaded glass windows featuring the Masonic emblem. The Masonic Widows and Orphans Home Historic District (the earlier name for the facility) was listed in the National Register of Historic Places in 1992. ⊛

MASONIC HOME AND SCHOOL OF TEXAS/ADMINISTRATION BUILDING

129

Cattle, railroad, and oil interests were the major players in Fort Worth's economy during the early years of the twentieth century, but cotton and other agricultural products had supporting roles. Neil P. Anderson (1847-1912) established Fendley, Anderson & Company (which later became Neil P. Anderson & Company), a cotton brokerage firm, by 1882 shortly after his arrival in Fort Worth. After Anderson's death in 1912, operations were continued by his son Bernie Anderson (d. 1961) and son-in-law, Morris Berney (1873-1948).

In 1919, the two men purchased Sam Levy's homestead at the corner of West Seventh and Lamar streets. The site, located where Seventh Street curves, acts as a gateway to the central business district. They commissioned Sanguinet and Staats to draw plans for the building that would house Neil P. Anderson & Company, the Fort Worth Cotton and Grain Exchange, United States Agriculture Department offices, numerous other grain and cotton merchants, and first-floor retail operations. W. C. Hedrick Construction Company run by Wyatt C. Hedrick, an architect and engineer who would later join Sanguinet and Staats and buy the firm when they retired in 1925, was the project contractor.

Distinguished by a graceful curving facade that overlooks nearby Burnett Park, the eleven-story buff-brick building has distinctive terra cotta ornamentation including medallions depicting bales of cotton and stems of grain, panels with garland swags, and paired urns which top the parapet wall. Curved windows, on the building's curved bay which meets the bend in Seventh Street, are unusual in Fort Worth. The storefront windows were large plate glass panes set in bronze. Inside, the office floors had marble wainscoting, wood and glass partitions, and red tile floors. The top floor of the building was a cotton sample showroom where cotton could be graded according to texture and color. Enormous skylights on this level provide natural north light, necessary for accurate inspection and grading.

Neil P. Anderson & Company closed in 1939, but the building remained in the family. A 1959 renovation by Herman Cox, architect, and Ellis Brown, contractor, included the application of an aluminum fascia over the facade of the first two floors, redesign of the storefront windows, and remodeling of the lobby entrance. Other interior remodeling, also handled by Cox and Brown, took place in 1965, two years after the Anderson family sold the building to R. G. Hughes.

The building had numerous owners between 1963 and 1977 when it was purchased by 411 Company Ltd. in a last-minute effort to prevent demolition. The lender had foreclosed on the building, evicted the remaining tenants, and begun plans to tear it down. The 411 Company Ltd., led by Charles W. Rogers, hired architect Martin Growald to restore the building's facade and adapt the interior space for contemporary office use. Rogers served as the contractor for the project which has given the building a new life. The Neil P. Anderson Building was listed in the National Register of Historic Places and designated as a Recorded Texas Historic Landmark in 1978. ⊛

NEIL P. ANDERSON BUILDING

NEIL P. ANDERSON BUILDING

SANGER BROTHERS BUILDING/SANGER LOFTS AT SUNDANCE SQUARE

*D*allas-based Sanger Brothers, a department store, expanded their operations to Fort Worth in 1918. The brothers, Alex and Philip Sanger, were shrewd merchants who built a chain of stores based on innovative merchandising, public service, civic involvement, and employee relations. In 1924-1925, Sanger Brothers erected a new store building at 515 Houston Street, just down the street from the future site of this building. Citing the need for additional space, the company in 1928 began construction on this five-story commercial building with Spanish Revival detailing.

The 90,000 square-foot building occupies one-third of a city block and fronts on Throckmorton, West Fourth, and Houston streets. It was designed by Fort Worth architect Wyatt C. Hedrick and built by Wohlfield and Witt, local contractors. There were numerous problems during construction of the $1 million building, including the collapse of a wall and two fires in the adjacent J. C. Penney store. Pre-opening publicity noted that 500 tons of stone, twenty-nine tons of granite, 380 tons of steel, forty miles of wiring, and an acre of glass were used in the building. The lighting was said to have enough candlepower to illuminate the entire town of Weatherford. Publicity touted the store's "manufactured weather"– not just heating, which was common – but air conditioning, a new luxury. The ground floor storefronts have fluted concrete pilasters, shallow rectangular columns projecting only slightly from the wall, and entrance doors topped by elaborate flat metal canopies. On the second through fifth floors, tall pilasters with ornate capitals alternate with pairs of windows – emphasizing the vertical design of the building.

At the grand opening on June 25, 1929, few persons were thinking about the impending economic collapse that would soon grip the country. The Depression took its toll, nonetheless, and the store closed in 1930 not long after it had opened. Sangers did not return to Fort Worth until 1977 when the Sanger Harris (now Foley's) store opened at Hulen Mall.

The building stood vacant through the 1930s, but in 1943 was renovated by the firm of Clarkson, Pelich, Geren and Rady for use as a U.S.O. (United Service Organizations) facility for soldiers. It was the largest U.S.O. in the United States and housed sleeping quarters, recreational facilities, and a basement canteen. In 1946, J. C. Penney Co. purchased the building and moved here from their store next door. The storefront display windows were altered at this time, and the interior was renovated for store use. Penney's operated here until 1970, and the building had a variety of tenants after that time. Sundance Square, Inc. purchased the building in 1981, and the eastern section of the first floor served as the flagship store for Pier 1 Imports between 1986 and 1992. The Fort Worth Convention and Visitors Bureau currently has its offices on the western side of the building at 415 Throckmorton Street.

In the late 1980s, interest grew in downtown housing for Fort Worth. Sundance Square, Inc., determined that the open configuration of the upper floors of the Sanger Brothers Building made it a good candidate for conversion as loft apartments. Sanger Lofts at Sundance Square opened in 1993. The renovation project was designed by David M. Schwarz Architects and construction was handled by Linbeck Construction. The Sanger Brothers Building was listed in the National Register of Historic Places in 1994. ⊛

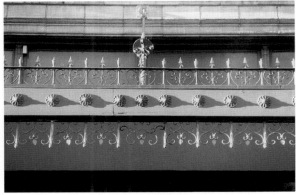

*N*oted Fort Worth architect Joseph R. Pelich designed this house for Eunice and Simon W. Freese. Located on a large bluff-top site just north of Texas Christian University, the residence is a handsome limestone-veneered building that is well integrated with the wooded lot on which it stands. Pelich drew plans for many houses and schools in Fort Worth during the 1920s and 1930s, but the Freese House is one of his best. Eclectic design, blending various historic European styles, was popular during this time period. Although Pelich's design evokes no specific style, it does blend elements from Tudor and Chateauesque period designs in a pleasing manner. H. T. Mangham was the contractor for the project.

Simon Wilke Freese (1900-1990) trained as an engineer at the Massachusetts Institute of Technology, graduated with a degree in civil engineering in 1921, and came to Fort Worth in 1922 to work for John B. Hawley, founder of a company that specialized in developing water resources. Freese became Hawley's partner in 1927 and the business was renamed Hawley, Freese and Nichols when Marvin C. Nichols associated with the company in 1930. Hawley retired in 1937, and the firm became Freese and Nichols. Over the years, the company had a hand in developing water supplies for fifty Texas communities as well as the design and construction of many flood control, road, bridge, and railroad projects. Freese has been widely regarded as one of the 'water pioneers of Texas' for his work to ensure that areas of Texas which did not have sufficient natural water resources to support farming, ranching, and industry had enough water to make those ventures possible.

Both Freese and his wife, Eunice, were active in civic affairs. He served on the Fort Worth school board from 1931-1941 and was responsible for selecting the architects for many of the school buildings built during that time. Eunice Freese, an active club woman and genealogist, also served on the first grand jury in Tarrant County which empaneled women. After her death in 1985, Simon Freese continued to work on projects for the firm and began to write the centennial history of Freese and Nichols entitled *A Century in the Works: Freese and Nichols Consulting Engineers, 1894-1994*. With the assistance of co-author Deborah L. Sizemore, the book was published in posthumously in 1994. The house was sold in 1990, following Simon Freese's death. ⊛

FREESE HOUSE

*P*ark Hill, a neighborhood over-looking Forest Park, has wide, curving streets and substantial stone-and brick-clad homes built in the late 1920s for Fort Worth's business and professional leaders. In October 1928, Mabel and V. T. Bolin contracted with Model Home Builders, Inc., a firm which built a number of Park Hill residences, to erect this house according to plans drawn by local architect James C. Teague. The Bolins apparently never lived here, because in September 1929 they sold the house to W. C. Guthrie, the man who developed the Park Hill Addition. A little more than a month later, Fort Worth attorney William A. Hanger (1869-1944) and his wife Mattie purchased the house.

Hanger, one of Fort Worth's most prominent lawyers, was born in a log cabin in Forest Hill and lived most of his life in Tarrant County. He practiced law for fifty-four years, and his firm, known at the time of his death as Cantey, Hanger, McMahon, McKnight, and Johnson, is still in business today as Cantey & Hanger. Hanger had a life-long interest in politics and political history, but he put his beliefs into practice serving as a state senator from 1898 to 1906. Both of the Hangers were involved in a number of civic organizations. Mattie Hanger served as the first female president of the Fort Worth Library Association, while her husband was a director of the Fort Worth Exposition and Fat Stock Show.

Mrs. Hanger continued to live here after her husband died in 1944, occupying the house until her own death in 1967 when it was sold to Claire and John Armstrong, a physician. Rickey J. Brantley, also an attorney, purchased the house in 1991.

Located on a curving hilltop site, this romantically-styled buff-brick house has a red Spanish tile roof. Arched or arcaded porches and terraces on the southern end of the house and the decorative corbel table or projecting blocks running just below the eaves on the front gable give the eclectic house a Romanesque Revival air. The square tower, with a third story room at its top, also adds to the home's picturesque charm. ⊛

HANGER HOUSE

137

*A*lthough Dr. William C. Lackey bought this triangular Park Hill lot in 1928, he did not build his home here until 1933. The records are not clear but it appears that Lackey, a physician who maintained his office in the Medical Arts Building, and his wife Elizabeth commissioned Ben B. Milam to draw plans for their home. Milam was a local architect well-versed in residential Tudor Revival design. B. B. Adams, a prominent local contractor who built many of Fort Worth's bungalow fire stations during the early 1920s, constructed the house.

Lackey died in 1946, and in 1949 the residence was purchased by Virginia and Thomas T. Chamberlain. An actuary, Chamberlain served as chief actuary of Prudential Insurance Company's Texas insurance department before becoming vice-president of Tillinghast, Nelson and Warren, Inc., a financial services company, in 1976. He was active in the Actuaries' Club of the Southwest as well as in several local social organizations. Mrs. Chamberlain took part in community theater activities. The Chamberlains sold the house in 1965, and it has had a number of owners since.

Located on a tight bend where Medford Court East meets Medford Court West, the enchanting Tudor Revival house has canted or angled bays that respond to the curving site. Most of the house is clad in finely laid limestone blocks, but a portion of the second story has half-timbering with a rich yellow brick infill. The massive stone chimney, steeply pitched roof, and cast-stone trim around Tudor-arched windows further add to the charm of the residence. ⊛

LACKEY HOUSE

*D*allas architect Charles Stevens Dilbeck is well known for his picturesque Period Revival houses which have a distinctive storybook air. Dilbeck designed this house for I. C. Parker (1899-1976), an executive with Fort Worth's Pangburn Company, a candy manufacturer.

Parker began his career with the Pangburn Ice Cream and Candy Co. in 1926 and in 1931 was credited with the invention of the frozen drumstick when a peanut-covered ice cream cone fell into a vat of chocolate. His wife, Jewel, gave the confection its name because she thought it looked like a frozen drumstick. Jewel Parker was a commercial artist who drew the "pin-up" cowgirls that became the symbol for Pangburn's Western Style Chocolates, and she was also responsible for the art work for the original Casa Manana, Billy Rose's 1936 theatrical extravaganza celebrating the Texas Centennial. In 1943, Parker became president of the Pangburn Company, a position he held until his retirement in 1970. At the time of his death in 1976, he was chairman of the board.

This fanciful rock house has a commanding view of Fort Worth from its bluff-top site west of Texas Christian University. The house was built in 1937 of native stone dug from the lot when the foundation was excavated. According to family information, German-born contractor Clyde E. Shankle of Dallas built the house with the assistance of his five sons. Dilbeck's storybook features include a round stair tower with a conical roof, a balcony supported by log brackets, and a shake roof. Inside, the living room features a massive fireplace which holds four-foot logs and is made of specially shaped and fired rounded bricks which resemble ballast stones. The living room has oak flooring and ceiling beams, while several other rooms have ceiling beams or cabinets made of pecky or 'worm-eaten' cypress. The tower stairway is constructed of massive stacked oak planks held together without nails, screws, or bolts.

Although Charles Dilbeck designed several buildings in the Fort Worth area, including the Meadowmere Apartments on Birchman and Pershing avenues, the Griffith House on Westridge Avenue, the Abbott House on Spanish Trail, and the two Meeker homes – one in River Oaks and the other on Crestwood Drive – he is best known for the hundreds of houses he designed in Highland Park, University Park, and in the Lakewood area of Dallas during the 1930s and 1940s. His rambling designs combine a medley of materials and eccentric detailing which often give the buildings a rustic appearance. Contemporary houses left him cold. Dilbeck felt that "a house should say, 'Welcome. Come in, sit down and enjoy yourself.'" The Parker House was designated as a City of Fort Worth Landmark in 1993. ⊛

*I*n announcing the anticipated completion of the new Elks Lodge building early in 1928, Chairman Harry G. Brickhouse noted that "the Elks Club is something more than a club house. It is an expression on the part of the Elks of Fort Worth of the desire to contribute to the means of getting comfort and happiness out of life in this, our home city." The club building, located on the western side of Fort Worth's central business district, was clearly designed to be a comfortable and traditional home-away-from-home for Elks Club members. Built of cream-colored brick and cast stone with wrought iron railings and balconies, the five story building has an almost residential-style front entry porch with a balcony.

The building was designed by Wyatt C. Hedrick, Architects and Engineers, and erected by Thomas S. Byrne, Inc., Engineers and Contractors. While the exterior is in a restrained Georgian or Colonial Revival style, the interior is decidedly less controlled with a Spanish Eclectic first floor lounge featuring beautiful stenciled ceilings and a second floor Georgian lodge room (now a ballroom) and ladies' parlors. When the building was new, the basement housed a kitchen, gymnasium, dining rooms, and barber shop and the upper floors contained furnished rooms available to both resident and non-resident members. The grand opening was held May 7-9, 1928.

By the early 1950s, the Elks decided they wanted a club building further away from the central business district and sold this building, in 1954, to the YWCA. The YWCA has continued to use the upper floors of the building for residential purposes, offering a supportive living program and special needs child care as well as classes and recreational activities. In 1990 the Historic Preservation Council's Designer Showcase was held at the YWCA and substantial rehabilitation work was undertaken. Local architect Paul Koeppe prepared the preservation plan for the building and oversaw the preservation efforts. The Elks Lodge/YWCA Building was listed in the National Register of Historic Places in 1984. It was designated as a Recorded Texas Historic Landmark in 1986 and as a City of Fort Worth Landmark in 1991. ⊛

ELKS LODGE/YWCA

ELKS LODGE/YWCA

ELKS LODGE/YWCA

145

With its twin Gothic towers reaching skyward, First United Methodist Church is a landmark on the western edge of Fort Worth's central business district. Previously housed in a 1908 church building in the heart of downtown, the congregation grew from 1,106 members in 1906 to 3,034 in 1931, making larger quarters essential. First Methodist purchased the land for this building in 1928 and selected local architect Wiley G. Clarkson to draw plans for the new church. Harry B. Friedman was the contractor for the $1 million project.

Clarkson, who designed in a variety of styles – as evidenced by his work on the nearby Masonic Temple and Cook Children's Hospital, – chose the Gothic Revival style for First Methodist's new home. His design, with a triple portal entrance, pier buttresses on the corner towers, and three-story arrangement, draws its inspiration from Notre Dame in Paris. The church is constructed of buff brick with delicate Gothic terra cotta tracery, tall lancet windows, and an arcade of marble-filled arches on the front facade. As with the Gothic cathedrals of Europe, details are carefully incorporated into the balance of the overall design.

Ground was broken on the eve of the Depression, October 29, 1929, and one year later, on October 30, 1930, members locked the doors of the old church at Seventh and Taylor and marched together to the new building. Work had not quite been completed, however, and formal opening ceremonies were delayed until June 14, 1931. The large sanctuary with painted faux stone walls was not the only place where services were held. During the early years the church did not have air conditioning, and on warm summer evenings folding chairs were placed in the cloistered courtyard so that the minister could lead services from a stone pulpit in the sanctuary wall. The courtyard was planted as the Garden Garth in 1956, after air conditioning was installed.

First Methodist has thrived, and several harmonious additions have been made to the church complex through the years, including Epworth Hall constructed in 1954-1955 and the Armstrong Children's Wing built in 1969-1970. In March 1965 a new Reuter organ was installed in the main sanctuary. With 105 ranks and 6,610 pipes it was, at that time, the largest organ made by the Reuter Organ Company. Many influential Fort Worth families have attended First Methodist, and it continues to play a major role in the religious life of the community. ⊕

FIRST UNITED METHODIST CHURCH

FIRST UNITED METHODIST CHURCH

FIRST UNITED METHODIST CHURCH

149

*W*hen cattleman and developer C. A. O'Keefe announced plans for his new hotel building on March 25, 1928, the *Fort Worth Star-Telegram* noted that the design "... resembles many of the latest hotels which have been constructed in New York, Chicago and Saint Louis." The style of the city's first Art Deco skyscraper was said to be "modern design, purely American" in its vertical set-back form. It was another sign that Fort Worth wanted to make its mark as a major urban hub rather than simply act as a regional center.

Local architect Elmer Withers worked with the Saint Louis firm of Mauran, Russell and Crowell, which had extensive experience in designing Texas luxury hotels (see Hotel Texas), to draw plans for the building. Constructed by the Bellows-Maclay Construction Company, the fireproof reinforced concrete building is covered with buff-colored brick and terra cotta trim. Although the overall form of the building is a stepped-back or ziggurat skyscraper, much of the original detailing and interior design was more traditional, following Renaissance, Gothic, and Italianate models. As built, the hotel had twenty-two floors containing 284 guest rooms. Luxury suites, on the fifteenth and eighteenth floors, opened onto awning-covered terraces.

From the time it opened, the Blackstone was a focal point of the Fort Worth social scene. Prominent guests included Clark Gable, D. W. Griffith, Lawrence Welk, Benny Goodman, and every president from Herbert Hoover to Richard Nixon. Bob Wills recorded the hit song "San Antonio Rose" in the WBAP radio studios on the twenty-second floor of the hotel, and his Light Crust Doughboys regularly broadcast from the studio.

In 1952, the Hilton Hotel Corporation leased the Blackstone Hotel, took over its operations, and renamed it the Hilton. The corporation remodeled the hotel, "modernizing" the ground floor facade and lobby and constructing an addition south of the main hotel building. Hilton's management agreement terminated in 1962, however, and the hotel was again operated as the Blackstone. By this time, Fort Worth's central business district was beginning to decline, and the hotel never regained the popularity of its first decades. Twice, in 1964 and 1986, the hotel was sold at foreclosure auctions on the steps of the Tarrant County Courthouse, and it has seen many owners in the past three decades. The hotel closed in 1982, purportedly for remodeling, but did not reopen. The small size of the rooms and solid concrete construction have made adaptive reuse options difficult. In 1994, the building was vacant with plans for its renovation still uncertain. The Blackstone Hotel was listed in the National Register of Historic Places in 1984 and designated as a City of Fort Worth Landmark in 1990. ⊛

BLACKSTONE HOTEL

BLACKSTONE HOTEL

BLACKSTONE HOTEL

153

Oilman Edward A. Landreth (1881-1962) and his wife Adele built this imposing mansion on a three-and-one-half-acre site near Rivercrest Country Club in 1928. Landreth, president of the Landreth Production Company which he established in 1918, made his initial fortune in West Texas oil fields during the 1920s. He moved to Fort Worth shortly before he sold his interests in a Crane County field called "The Landreth Strip," the Hendrick Field in Winkler County, and several million barrels of oil which he had stored, because there had been no market, to The Texas Company (which later became Texaco) for $6.5 million in June of 1928.

Landreth hired the noted Dallas architectural firm of Fooshee and Cheek (Marion F. Fooshee and James B. Cheek) to draw plans for his house. Among the firm's more notable Dallas commissions are the Highland Park Shopping Village, Hillcrest Mausoleum, and John B. Hood Junior High School, as well as many Highland Park residences.

The architects designed a romantic two-and-one-half-story Tudor Revival home clad in polychrome sandstone with stuccoed half-timbering in the front gables and red brick framing around the windows. It is less an historically accurate evocation of Tudor architecture than Tudoresque detailing used in a symmetrical, almost classical arrangement. A Tudor-arched cast-stone portal frames the main entry, and the roof is covered with polychrome slate tiles. The colorful exuberance of the house is enhanced by its massive scale, and it has a commanding presence overlooking the bend in Rivercrest Road.

Despite significant losses in the stock market crash of 1929 and a number of dry wells drilled during the 1930s, Landreth also had successes that ensured his prosperity. In 1940-1941, he sold most of his oil interests and retired but continued a strong interest in education and in civic projects. The Ed Landreth Fine Arts Building at Texas Christian University is named for Landreth, and he served on the university's Board of Trustees from 1946 until his death in 1962. In 1943, the Landreths sold their Rivercrest home to Alice and Kenneth W. Davis (1895-1968), another major figure in Fort Worth's oil business.

Davis went to work for Mid-Continent Supply Company, an oil-field equipment company, in 1929 and by the late 1930s had expanded its services worldwide. Mid-Continent would eventually become the world's largest independent supplier of drilling rigs and other oil-field supplies. Under the umbrella of Kendavis Industries International, Inc., Davis also operated a number of other drilling, manufacturing, truck-heavy equipment, and supply concerns. His sons, Kenneth William, Jr., T. Cullen, and William S. Davis, were also active in the family's business interests. Like Landreth, Kenneth W. Davis was also active in charitable and civic causes. He provided funds for the Noble Planetarium at the Fort Worth Children's Museum (now the Fort Worth Museum of Science and History) as well as for organizations that work with young people, including the Girl Scouts, YMCA, and Campfire Girls. Davis died in 1968, but the house remains in the family. ⊛

LANDRETH-DAVIS HOUSE

LANDRETH-DAVIS HOUSE

157

Sited on a bluff overlooking the West Fork of the Trinity River, this Crestline Road residence was designed by Houston architect John F. Staub for candy manufacturer John P. King (1861-1946) and his wife Lorena. The 1928 house was not the first in the area – the Williams-Penn House next door was built in 1908 and the Baldridge House at 5100 Crestline Road in 1910-1913 – but the Colonial Revival residence has a stately presence in this neighborhood of large and imposing homes. At first, the house seems to be typical of the Colonial Revival style – a symmetrical design divided into five bays by pilasters, front door with a decorative broken pediment, and double-hung sash windows with multi-pane glazing topped by a louvered fan motif and flanked by shutters – but the front facade conceals an asymmetrical house in which the main entrance is actually off the porte-cochere on the west side of the residence. The design is obviously a concession to the automobile age, not a historically accurate recreation.

John P. King moved from Brenham to Fort Worth with his family when he was about eight years old. As a young man, he worked in a dry goods store and served as Tarrant County Clerk for several years. In 1906, he founded the King Candy Company, which eventually distributed its sweet wares throughout the southern United States. The firm's King Candy Store and Tearoom, located on Houston Street during the 1920s, was fondly remembered by many shoppers for the delightful treats it offered after a hard day spent in the downtown department stores. King also had interests in the Southern Cold Storage and Produce Company, Universal Ford Sales Company, and Mount Olivet Cemetery and served as president of the Fort Worth Chamber of Commerce.

By the time the Kings built this house, Mr. King was sixty-seven years of age and enjoying the benefits of his business success. Visitors to the house recall that it was furnished with the finest French, English, and American antiques, a tradition carried on by the second owners, Ella C. and William H. McFadden, the head of Southland Royalty Company, who purchased the residence in 1938. Mrs. McFadden continued to live here following her husband's death in 1956, and it was sold after her death in 1965 to Betty Claire and Robert Dupree, a banker. In 1982, continuing the tradition of graceful and elegant living established by the home's previous owners, the Duprees allowed the Historic Preservation Council to use their home as the second Designer Showhouse. ⊛

KING-McFADDEN-DUPREE HOUSE

159

*H*oward Barnstone, architect John F. Staub's biographer, attributed Staub's design for Elizabeth and Herman Gartner's house to "European-influenced eclecticism" encouraged by a European study trip that the architect made during the summer of 1929 as preparation for a commission to design a house for Nenetta Carter, wife of Amon G. Carter. Although Carter's residence was never built, the Houston-based Staub became fascinated with the Dutch-style brickwork and gables that he saw in southern England; the oversized Flemish gable that fronts the Gartner House is a direct result of that inspiration.

Herman W. Gartner (1886-1965) moved to Fort Worth from Dallas in 1909 to enter the insurance business and was soon a principal in the firm of Mitchell, Gartner and Walton. In 1914, Gartner married Elizabeth Reynolds, daughter of pioneer cattleman George W. Reynolds, and in 1929, the couple commissioned Staub to design this house, which faces Rivercrest Country Club. Fort Worth contractor B. B. Adams completed the $60,000 residence in 1930.

Staub's complex design hides the fact that the house is really laid out to face south, not west as the front entry suggests Behind the undulating gable, with its inset decorative metal screen, the rooms open off an axial spine, with changes in floor level to accommodate the site terrain. The house is faced in a warm, variegated red brick laid in Flemish bond, and the roof is clad in ceramic tile. The porte-cochere to the north was a later addition designed by Staub. The fine interior detailing is classical in design, reflecting an even more conservative taste than the somewhat fanciful facade.

The Gartners lived here until 1938 when C. J. Wrightman, president of Wrightman Oil Company, purchased the house. Wrightman and his wife Edna occupied the house until 1960, when it was acquired by Marshall R. Young (1894-1976), also an oilman. In 1926, Young's company, then called Roeser and Pendleton and later the Marshall R. Young Oil Company, discovered oil on the Cook Ranch near Albany. Mrs. Cook used the royalties from this endeavor to fund the W. I. Cook Memorial Hospital (see Cook Children's Hospital), and Young served on the hospital board for many years. Young was also active in several petroleum industry associations and helped to found the Texas Boys Choir and the All Church Home. Following Young's death, the house was occupied for a time by his son, Frank G. Young, who served as vice-president of the Marshall R. Young Oil Company. The house remains in the family. ⊛

J. Marvin Leonard (1895-1970), better known throughout his life as "Mr. Marvin," was a quintessential Fort Worth businessman who developed innovative retail merchandising techniques and had a flair for finding markets for goods when no one else saw the potential. When a manufacturer practically gave away 2,000 pair of bright red trousers, Leonard bought the pants, dressed his sales people in them, and held a special sale. Soon, Leonard said, "the whole town was in red pants."

Leonard opened his first store in Fort Worth in 1918 and shortly thereafter joined with his brother, Obie Leonard, to form Leonard Brothers, a general merchandise and department store located on the block bounded by Throckmorton, First, Houston, and Second streets. The establishment sold everything from groceries to automobile supplies to ready-to-wear. Leonard Brothers even installed its own free subway system which ran from a parking lot on the Trinity River to the store. In 1967, Leonard Brothers sold its property and assets to the Tandy Corporation. Tandy built Tandy Center on the site of the old store, preserving the famed subway system.

Retailing was not Leonard's only passion. Fond of golf, he built Shady Oaks Country Club and established the Colonial National Invitation Golf Tournament. Leonard was also active in insurance, real estate, and banking and developed the Ridgmar Addition.

With his wife Mary, Leonard built this Rivercrest home overlooking the Rivercrest Country Club golf course about 1935. Fort Worth developer A. C. Luther of Byrne & Luther, Inc., who was responsible for constructing many residences in Rivercrest and Westover Hills as well as the Ridglea Village Shopping Center, built the home. The picturesque Tudor Revival residence is clad in a warm orange brick with a diaper patterning on the south cross-gabled wing and has a polychrome slate roof. The north wing has a bowed bay with a roof terrace and three enormous stepped chimneys flank the main hip-roofed section of the house. Set on a manicured lawn with a brick garden wall and mature landscape, the vine-covered home is both imposing in its scale and intimate in its picturesque detail. The house remains in the Leonard family. ⊛

LEONARD HOUSE

LEONARD HOUSE

LEONARD HOUSE

One of the last skyscrapers to be built in Fort Worth before the Depression tightened its grip, the Sinclair Building is also one of the best architectural monuments to the prosperity that the oil business brought Fort Worth. Oilman Richard Otto Dulaney (1882-1966), who built a landmark residence on Elizabeth Boulevard (see Dulaney House) in 1923 and constructed the Petroleum Building in 1927, bought this Main Street lot in July 1929 and announced plans to build a modern office tower. Dulaney, his architect Wiley G. Clarkson, and contractor Harry B. Friedman toured major cities in the north and east to look at the new buildings that were being designed and built.

Clarkson returned with plans to build the "most perfect type of modernistic architecture in the Southwestern states." Originally called the Dulaney Building, the name of the building was changed before completion because the Sinclair Oil Company leased seven of the sixteen floors. Other tenants have included the Northern Texas Traction Company, which ran the Fort Worth-Dallas Interurban, and a number of oil, law, and insurance firms.

Completed in 1930, the Sinclair Building is the best Zigzag Moderne structure in Fort Worth. The building is sixteen stories tall and built of Texas limestone and Minnesota granite. The top two stories are set back; eagle finials cap the green recessed window panels on the fourteenth floor, and as the structure steps back to form the fifteenth and sixteenth floors, the vertical mullions become exuberantly carved pinnacles. When illuminated at night, these details on the crown of the building make a dazzling statement. The building was built with two lobby entrances, one on Main Street and the other on West Fifth Street. A stepped or ziggurat motif used above the first floor windows is repeated in the entrances, and the Main Street entry has a striking Monel metal screen which introduces the Mayan Indian design motif repeated in other elements of the building's decoration.

Although the lobby area is small, its richly ornamented surfaces still dazzle the eye. Dark green marble walls, a tiered bronze- and silver-leaf plaster ceiling, and Moderne-style Monel elevator doors set in stepped portals all contribute to the opulent feel.

Over the years both the exterior and interior of the first floor were significantly altered, and many of the original decorative elements removed. In 1990 Ward Bogard and Associates, local architects, directed a restoration of the Sinclair Building. The decorative Monel entrance screens were recreated, and both exterior and interior lobby detailing restored or replaced. The crown of the building is once again dramatically lit at night. Johnny Pittman of Texas Sunshine, Inc., was the project construction manager. The Sinclair Building was listed in the National Register of Historic Places in 1992, designated as a Recorded Texas Historic Landmark in 1993 and as a City of Fort Worth Landmark in 1989. ⊛

SINCLAIR BUILDING

SINCLAIR BUILDING

*T*his small neighborhood service station is typical of gasoline-station design in Texas and the Southwest during the 1930s. Canopies were attached to the building (which housed the station office and garage bays) so that attendants and patrons could carry out their business with at least some degree of protection from the elements. The stucco-on-brick construction was more fireproof than earlier wood-frame stations, and the vague Mission detailing – red clay tile roof and decorative ceramic tile – was appropriate for the region.

Manvel Ervin (1892-1987) was Sinclair Refining Company's chief architect and engineer and was responsible for a five-state region which included Texas, New Mexico, Oklahoma, Arkansas, and Louisiana. He drew the plans that were used to build this station, as well as others of the same design in other locations within the region. This particular facility was operated by a number of individuals through the years as independent dealers for the Sinclair Refining Company. It opened in 1938 as the Buster and Jimmy Service Station, operated by Buster Mayes and James Journey. From the late 1940s through the 1950s it was called the Arlington Heights Service Station, for the adjacent neighborhood, and operated by Woodrow B. Stuart. The station closed in 1967 when Sinclair's Texas operations were acquired by Atlantic Richfield.

Manvel Ervin purchased the station he had designed, and the building remains in the family. It served as a radio store during the 1970s and 1980s, at which time it was painted bright yellow and the garage entrance sealed off. In 1988, Ervin's daughter restored the station and leased it for use as an automobile repair facility. Although the station is by no means the most extravagant of Fort Worth's remaining early gasoline stations, it is one of only a few that have not been extensively altered and it is an excellent example of the standardized station designs adopted by major oil companies. ✾

SINCLAIR GASOLINE STATION

TEXAS & PACIFIC WAREHOUSE BUILDING

172

$\mathcal{P}$UBLIC - PRIVATE ENDEAVORS • 1930s

During the late 1920s, the Fort Worth Chamber of Commerce proposed an ambitious Five Year Work Program to build $100 million worth of civic and business improvements. Voters passed bond issues, potential federal projects were identified, and private industry was given the word that its participation in this effort was needed to help transform Fort Worth into a major commercial center. Heading the list of projects was the completion of a new union railroad depot (see Texas & Pacific Passenger Terminal) and a major road building program. The stock market crash of October 29, 1929 occurred just as the program was getting off the ground but, rather than abandon the project, community leaders redoubled their efforts. As a result, by 1933 many of the Five Year Work Program goals had been accomplished, and Fort Worth was able to delay the devastating effects of the Depression. The variety and quality of buildings constructed during this period is remarkable.

$\mathcal{A}$lthough the Texas & Pacific Terminal and Warehouse structures, located on the southern edge of Fort Worth's central business district, are physically separated by the United States Post Office and Jennings Avenue, the buildings and the streets adjacent to them were part of a coordinated public/private project to improve rail service and to increase vehicular traffic between the central business district and the South Side.

On June 27, 1929, John L. Lancaster (for whom Lancaster Avenue is named), president of the Texas & Pacific Railway Company, and Fort Worth Mayor William Bryce (see Fairview and Bryce Building) announced a multi-million dollar project to construct a passenger terminal and a freight warehouse, and to separate the railroad tracks and streets by means of underpasses, overpasses, and street relocation. Because of cattle and oil operations, Fort Worth's railroads had prospered during the 1920s, and traffic was so heavy that new facilities were urgently needed. The Texas & Pacific committed $13 million to build the new terminal and warehouse as well as to expand local freight yards. For its part, the City of Fort Worth pledged $3 million to pay for street and track relocation and the construction of underpasses and overpasses. This effort was part of a five-year, ten-point program of capital improvements proposed by the Chamber of Commerce. Most of the work was completed by 1933, but some of the viaducts were not built until 1936-1937.

All parties were eager to move quickly, and by April of 1930 plans for the railroad buildings had

TEXAS & PACIFIC TERMINAL

been drawn and the project was put out for bid. Herman Paul Koeppe, chief designer for Wyatt C. Hedrick, designed both the terminal and warehouse, and Preston M. Geren was responsible for the structural plans. P. O'Brien Montgomery of Dallas was awarded the construction contract for both facilities. For Fort Worth, these major construction projects could not have come at a better time. The Depression was slowing building nationwide, and the jobs available on these projects, as well as on the construction of the nearby United States Post Office, helped blunt the devastating effect of economic collapse. The passenger terminal opened on October 25, 1931, serving four railroad lines: Texas & Pacific, Fort Worth & Denver City, International-Great Northern, and the Missouri-Kansas-Texas.

Both buildings are stunning examples of Zigzag Moderne architecture. The passenger terminal, constructed of brick trimmed with limestone, terracotta, and marble, is twelve stories tall with a mezzanine and a basement. Above the three-story granite and limestone base (two levels plus the mezzanine), the ten-story main rectangular block has rows of windows recessed in vertical panels and flanking corner towers, projecting slightly from the central core, which are capped by octagonal drums. Opulent ornamentation, including geometric designs, plant forms, urns, spiraling scrolls, and eagles, abounds on both the exterior and interior of the building.

Most of the public rail facilities – waiting rooms (originally there were three waiting rooms, the main area for whites flanked by smaller rooms for white women and African-Americans), ticket offices, restrooms, restaurant, and concourse – are on the first level; the Texas & Pacific maintained offices on the third floor. The remainder of the office space, reached via an office building lobby on the west end, was lease

space. A few transportation-related entities, such as the Pullman Company, Missouri Pacific Lines, and the Southwest Warehouse and Transfermen's Association, located here along with a handful of other concerns, but most of the office space was vacant until World War II. The United States Army Air Force Flying Training Command then took the ninth through twelfth floors, and the army's Finance Office leased the fifth floor. Other governmental offices followed after the war.

Off the concourse, to the south of the main building, underground tunnels led to the train tracks and additional facilities including a telegraph office, checkroom, barber shop, and cafe for African-Americans. The main waiting room measures ninety by sixty feet with a thirty-four-foot cast-plaster ceiling finished in gold leaf, silver leaf, and enamel. Fluted pilasters, marble flooring and wainscot, eleven frosted glass chandeliers, aluminum window frames with etched designs, and metal grilles complete this exquisite room.

The Texas & Pacific Warehouse, which also opened in 1931, is a mammoth eight-story building, located one block west of the terminal building, which handled inbound freight. Although its design is simpler than the Texas & Pacific Terminal building, the warehouse has a similar massing and is constructed of brick with limestone and tile trim. An enormous building, 611 feet long by 100 feet wide, the facility contained office space for freight companies, general merchandise storage, cold storage (on the west end, the area without windows), and showrooms. It was also designed by Herman Paul Koeppe working for Wyatt C. Hedrick and constructed by P. O'Brien Montgomery.

The Texas & Pacific Terminal operated until March 22, 1967, when the last train, the Texas & Pacific Eagle, pulled into the station from El Paso. In 1978, both the terminal and warehouse buildings were

purchased by the Merchants Terminal Corporation owned by Halden Connor and John O'Hara. Vacant for twelve years, the passenger terminal was finally resurrected as an office building in 1978, with most of the space leased to the Department of Housing and Urban Development. In 1981, Connor and O'Hara terminated their partnership with Connor taking control of the terminal and O'Hara the warehouse.

The Texas & Pacific Terminal and Warehouse buildings were listed in the National Register of Historic Places in 1978, and the terminal was designated as a Recorded Texas Historic Landmark in 1980. Along with their other National Register-listed neighbors (see the United States Post Office and the Public Market Building) the terminal and warehouse buildings were threatened by the Texas Highway Department's plans to widen the Interstate-30 overhead freeway, originally constructed in 1958, located just to the north. A lawsuit, filed by I-CARE (Citizen Advocates for Responsible Expansion), and mediation persuaded the state to reroute I-30 about 700 feet to the south along Vickery Boulevard and rebuild Lancaster Avenue as a boulevard.

Several proposals have been made for redevelopment of the warehouse building, including use as a luxury office and shopping complex or as housing, but to date none have proved viable. Plans call for railroad activity to return to the Texas & Pacific Terminal as a result of its 1993 designation as an intermodal transportation center. The proposed complex will house many forms of transportation including Amtrak, commuter rail, bus line, auto rental, and airline ticketing facilities in the Texas & Pacific Terminal under this federal program intended to create a new type of passenger hub facility. ⊛

TEXAS & PACIFIC TERMINAL/WAITING ROOM

TEXAS & PACIFIC TERMINAL

TEXAS & PACIFIC TERMINAL/CONCOURSE

TEXAS & PACIFIC TERMINAL/CAFE

*M*onumental civic buildings provide a place to organize and deliver government services, but they also serve an important function as community symbols – a representation of the character of the people those structures serve. Fort Worth's historic main post office, constructed during the early years of the Depression, is a remarkable building not only for its excellent architectural design but also for the way in which it represents the icons of the city's past.

Postal service was established in Fort Worth in 1856, when Julian Feild was named the first postmaster. Until the construction of a red sandstone post office and federal building on Jennings Avenue at 11th in 1896, local postal service had operated out of a succession of buildings in the downtown area. That facility served residents for thirty-six years, but a growing demand for postal services (receipts increased from $75,510.45 in 1900 to $1,650,682.11 in 1930) drove the need for a new post office building. The decision was made to locate the new facility near the Texas & Pacific Passenger Terminal since most incoming and outgoing mail was handled by railroads that used the station, and the federal government purchased the site for the new post office from the T&P.

Wyatt C. Hedrick received the commission to design the building. Hedrick worked with Joseph J. Patterson, also from Fort Worth, on the plans for the post office. Ralph Sollitt & Sons of Chicago were the general contractors for the project; Tom Archer and Company, a Fort Worth firm, handled the excavation work. Ground for the new postal facility was broken on August 11, 1931, and the formal dedication of the building was held on February 22, 1933.

Occupying a full city block, the post office is an imposing building constructed of Cordova limestone quarried near Austin. The rectangular, temple-plan three-story building sits over a granite-faced, partially-raised basement with a light well. It draws much of its inspiration from Beaux Arts design which favored large structures with extensive classical details. A colonnade of sixteen unfluted classical columns with elaborate capitals featuring Texas Longhorn and Polled Hereford cattle stretches the length of the front facade. The cattle motifs are marvelous adaptations of the icons of Fort Worth's frontier origins and the cattle trade to the more typical use of classical design elements, and they give the building a strong regional identity. The cornice is ornamented with carvings of lion heads.

The most striking room in the post office is the marble-lined lobby which runs the length of the building. Coffered or recessed ceiling panels are embellished with gold leaf and a rich dark green paint which complements the marble and bronze interior scheme. Pendant light fixtures with frosted glass globes once provided illumination, but most of these have been replaced by fluorescent fixtures. Several original glass-topped writing tables with elaborate bronze supports continue to serve the needs of postal patrons.

When the Jack D. Watson Station opened in 1986, this downtown facility ceased to serve as the central mail processing facility, but it continues to provide window and box service for customers. The building is proposed for redevelopment by the U. S. Post Office as a commercial office complex.

Before the elevated freeway was constructed in the 1950s, the post office, along with the Texas & Pacific Terminal and Warehouse buildings, provided a clear southern anchor for Fort Worth's central business district. Although the freeway has blocked the historic link those buildings had to the city's commercial center, current plans to re-route the freeway to the south and rebuild Lancaster Avenue as a boulevard will reestablish those important ties. The Fort Worth Post Office building was listed in the National Register of Historic Places in 1985 and designated as a Recorded Texas Historic Landmark in 1980. ⊛

UNITED STATES POST OFFICE

181

UNITED STATES POST OFFICE

UNITED STATES POST OFFICE/LOBBY

183

UNITED STATES POST OFFICE

Constructed on the eve of the Depression, the Fort Worth Public Market Building and its owners faced what would turn out to be insurmountable obstacles in an effort to provide residents with a centrally located farmers' market. John J. Harden, the Oklahoma City developer who financed and built the Spanish Colonial Revival market, spent over $150,000 to make the building a dramatic showplace that foreshadowed enclosed shopping malls in its grouping of retail establishments. The Public Market Building was designed by B. Gaylord Noftsger (1897-1979) of Oklahoma City, who had also designed market buildings for Harden in both Tulsa and Oklahoma City. Quisle and Andrews, a local firm, were the project contractors.

Despite the stock market crash of October 1929, the business scene in Fort Worth seemed promising through the early part of 1930 because of firm commitments to the city's five-year work program. Harden obtained his building permit in February 1930 and the building opened to the public on June 20 that same year.

The tan brick market is ornamented with glazed terra cotta tile and has a multi-colored red, orange, and green clay tile roof. The main portion of the building is square, with towers on three of its four corners. Located on the northeast corner of the building, the main tower is the most visible and highly ornamented portion of the building with decorative terra cotta columns and pilasters, a classical frieze, stained glass transom, and back-lit panels in the tower composed of a mosaic of multi-colored opaque and stained glass. This tower provided the primary entrance to the main building which housed commercial space for various retail businesses (grocers, bakers, and meat vendors) and a cold storage and food-cleaning area. The interior space was originally one open story with skylights in the center of the roof and a mezzanine, open to the central area, along the east and south walls. Very little of this interior arrangement remains intact today, as the space has been altered for various office and warehouse needs. The building housing the farmers' stalls wrapped around the western and southern sides of the main market.

Although the opening and early days of operation seemed successful, poor management and lax security coupled with the tightening economic visegrip of the Depression caused retail profit margins to disappear. In 1931, there were fourteen commercial operations and 132 farmers' stalls rented. By 1934, there were only six permanent concessions and twenty-three stall vendors. Harden was forced to transfer his interest in the project to the Public Market Company in 1932 and, although the company defaulted on its loans and lost the building, it continued to lease and manage the market until 1940. R. C. Bowen of Bowen Properties bought the building in 1944 and the company has leased it to a variety of tenants since.

When the Texas Department of Transportation planned the expansion of the elevated portion of Interstate 30 through downtown Fort Worth, the original design called for the demolition of the Public Market Building. Litigation and mediation resulted in the selection of an alternate route approximately 700 feet south of the current overhead that will retain the building. The Public Market Building was listed in the National Register of Historic Places in 1984 and designated as a Recorded Texas Historic Landmark in 1980. ⊛

PUBLIC MARKET BUILDING

PUBLIC MARKET BUILDING

*L*ocated just south of Texas Christian University, the Blue Bonnet Hills neighborhood is home to many Period Revival brick cottages, some with marvelous whimsical detailing. One of the most striking is the Mack-Ellman House which is often locally referred to as the 'Clock House' or 'Barometer House' because of the intriguing hands on the front facade.

The house was constructed in 1932 by builder Clifford A. Emery for the Blue Bonnet Hills Development Company, but the name of the architect has not been determined. After serving as a rental property for two years, the house was purchased by Jewell and Robert B. Mack, manager of the Fort Worth Wholesale Grocery and Produce Company, who lived here until 1939. Sara and Jack L. Ellman, owner of Peacock Jewelers, bought the house in 1939 and the couple lived here until his death in 1958. Mrs. Ellman continued to live in the house until she sold the property in 1963.

Built in a style sometimes called 'Mother Goose' architecture because of its fairy tale-like qualities, the Mack-Ellman House has a number of intersecting gables which project from the main body of the house and an abundance of decorative trim – from the scalloped bargeboards on the gables to the eccentric half-timbered band, to the metal hands set on stucco semi-circles above the doors and windows. No one knows whether the clock/barometer faces are original to the house or whether they may have been added by Jack Ellman as an inside joke on his trade as a jeweler. The house was designated as a City of Fort Worth Landmark in 1990. ❀

189

Shotgun houses are small one-story, wood-frame residences with gable fronts which are one room wide and two or more rooms deep. There is no hall, but each room opens into the adjacent room via a doorway in the shared wall. The term "shotgun" reportedly comes from the fact that a bullet fired through the front door of a shotgun house could exit the back door without piercing a wall. Often built without plans, these folk buildings were erected according to accepted tradition and practice. Economical to construct, shotguns were a common form of working-class housing in the urban South. Rows of identical shotgun houses constructed at the same time, such as these on East Oleander Street, were also frequent.

Cecil H. McBrayer purchased the property in July of 1938 and completed construction of these houses less than one month later. The seven three-room houses were erected at a cost of approximately $500 per unit and were rental dwellings. At the time, this was an African-American neighborhood, and it is likely that the early tenants were African-American. Among the first occupants were Vance Bennett, a laborer, Louis Hutchison, a chauffeur, Annie Johnson, a maid, and Ollie Prince, a boilermaker for the Texas & Pacific Railway.

Although Fort Worth has had good examples of shotgun houses in the past, many have been demolished in the face of redevelopment pressures or neighborhood decay. Others have been enlarged and remodeled to meet the needs of the families living in them. Single examples still exist, but few rows of shotguns survive in their original state or in reasonable condition. While the notion of the historic and architectural value of this type of housing may be difficult for some to appreciate – particularly those who lived in similar spartan circumstances when they had no other options – these houses are a fine example of vernacular, working-class housing for those who provided society's basic goods and services. ⊛

SHOTGUN HOUSES

*M*asonic organizations have been active in Fort Worth since April 1854 when Fort Worth Lodge No. 148 was organized. By the early 1920s there were several downtown-area lodges, congested meeting spaces, and a growing movement to erect a Masonic Temple – a single building which would house several Masonic bodies. William Stevenson Cooke, a local Masonic leader, led a committee that selected a four-block square site bounded by Texas Street, Henderson Street, Lancaster Avenue (then North Street), and Lake Street just west of downtown Fort Worth. The property was finally purchased in 1923, and a fund-raising campaign to build a $1 million dollar temple was undertaken in 1926.

Plans for the proposed building, designed by local architect Wiley G. Clarkson, show a mammoth Greek temple with a pedimented portico supported by massive columns. Fundraising proved to be more difficult than expected, and this design was never built. Local Masonic leaders toured other temple projects across the country and determined to scale the project back to a more manageable level – $600,000. The Depression made the project even more affordable when construction bids came in much lower than original estimates.

Clarkson's revised design was also classical in nature, a Classical Moderne building which incorporated a stepped-back temple form, massive Ionic columns, and the use of Masonic symbols in its design. The building, erected by contractor Harry B. Friedman, is both imposing and somewhat austere. Limestone columns on the top floor, decorative metal grilles, and etched stainless-steel doorways provide the major points of embellishment in the smooth-finished limestone facade. The doorway panels depict three Masters of Masonry who helped build King Solomon's Temple, and their impact is monumental to one who walks up the massive stairway leading to the front entrance. Befitting Masonic tradition, the building sits on an elevated site, faces east, and its overall design incorporates significant symbolic elements of the order. The grounds were originally landscaped by C. J. Dose.

Inside, the building design takes both a more classical and eclectic approach. Paul M. Heerwagen is credited with the interior design which includes a massive Gothic assembly room, an Arabian room for the Moslah Shrine, a walnut-paneled library, and Classical (Ionic, Doric and Corinthian) meeting rooms for the various lodges and Royal Arch chapters. Both the exterior and interior have seen relatively few changes since the building was constructed, and the Masons have taken particular pride in maintaining this impressive temple. In 1951, following the death of W. S. Cooke, the building was dedicated to him. The Masonic Temple was designated as a Recorded Texas Historic Landmark in 1984.⊛

MASONIC TEMPLE

193

MASONIC TEMPLE

MASONIC TEMPLE

*T*his building was originally a wood-frame church which housed the congregation of Holy Name Catholic Church. Holy Name was a new parish in 1909, established in the southeastern part of Fort Worth by the Right Reverend Edward J. Dunne, Bishop of the Diocese of Dallas which, at that time, included Fort Worth.

Father Bernard H. Diamond, the first priest at Holy Name, served until 1911, when he was replaced by Reverend John S. O'Conner. Father O'Conner was the priest at Holy Name from 1911 until his death in 1942, and it is to him that the church owes its current appearance. During O'Conner's tenure – sometime between 1926 and 1940, but most likely during the 1930s – the wood frame building was covered with stucco.

The church suffered a serious fire in November 1940 which damaged the building and destroyed most of its furnishings. It was rebuilt, however, and continued to serve Holy Name Church until 1952 when the congregation moved to a new location in order to gain more space. At that time, Our Mother of Mercy Parish moved here from Evans Avenue.

Established in 1929 by Father Narcissus Denis with about a dozen members, Our Mother of Mercy first held services in an abandoned drug store. Within two years, members of the African-American congregation built a new church and school and renovated another building for use as a convent. After the move to East Terrell, the church built a new school in 1958. A history compiled for the church's fifty-ninth anniversary notes that many leaders in the African-American community were educated at Our Mother of Mercy School and that many church leaders have been active in social justice and civil rights work. The congregation has continued to worship in and preserve this historic building.

The handsome Mission Revival building has a gabled roof and Mission or Alamo Revival-style parapets. The blocky composition, battered or sloping buttresses on the side elevations, and the stained glass windows give the rather small building a substantial air. ⊗

HOLY NAME CATHOLIC CHURCH/OUR MOTHER OF MERCY CATHOLIC CHURCH

*T*he North Holly Water Treatment Plant, named for the water pumping machinery produced by the Holly Manufacturing Company and used in the first facility here, is nestled between the Trinity River and the bluffs that flank the western edge of Fort Worth's central business district. Fort Worth began providing a municipal water supply in 1884 when it purchased a private company organized by B. B. Paddock in 1882. The growing population's demand for water soon outstripped the small pumping facility, and the city hired engineer John B. Hawley to manage construction of a new waterworks on this site in 1891-1892. Concurrent with the construction of Lake Worth, the city built its first water treatment facility here in 1911, with two sedimentation basins and four rapid sand filters.

Since that time, the city has maintained a carefully designed water treatment facility, utilizing compatible architectural styles and materials, at this location. Today, the core of the historic complex consists of a handsome Romanesque Revival wash water tank constructed in 1917 (moved across the complex in 1949) and a Mission Revival-style filter building constructed in 1932 with a 1952 addition. Other buildings in the North Holly complex generally date from the late 1940s and 1950s, and those in the South Holly plant after 1958.

Local architect Joseph R. Pelich designed the 1932 filter building, which was constructed by Frank Parrott and R. F. Ball; it contained a water filtration system designed by Hawley, Freese & Nichols. Hawley, who was intimately involved with all engineering aspects of Fort Worth's water system from 1891 until his retirement in 1937, was a guiding force in the layout and design of the North Holly Water Treatment Plant. Freese & Nichols, the successor firm (see Freese House), has handled the subsequent engineering design work for the facility.

The filter buildings, which form the strongest urban design feature in the complex, processed water piped from Lake Worth, Lake Bridgeport, and, after 1934, from Eagle Mountain Lake. Constructed of buff-colored brick, the Mission Revival structures have long, open-truss spaces filled with the sounds of running water. Marble-slab table tops and colorful tile mosaics complement the building's functional organization.

The North Holly Water Treatment Plant's park-like urban design and well-designed structures represent a tradition no longer common in municipal service facilities. Fort Worth's commitment to maintain this important complex and the rich community history it represents is significant to the overall understanding of the city's history. ✽

NORTH HOLLY WATER TREATMENT PLANT

NORTH HOLLY WATER TREATMENT PLANT

NORTH HOLLY WATER TREATMENT PLANT

*F*ort Worth benefitted from two large federal projects built during the early 1930s, the United States Post Office and the United States Courthouse, which was constructed on Tenth Street facing Burnett Park. Not only was the old Romanesque combination post office and courthouse built in 1892-1896 overcrowded, but the deepening Depression meant that Fort Worth was grateful for any projects that provided badly-needed jobs. Like other projects of this period, the courthouse became part of the city's Five Year Work Program, an ambitious effort to rebuild and improve Fort Worth's civic and business infrastructure.

Philadelphia architect Paul Philippe Cret, who enjoyed a nationwide reputation, was selected as the project architect. Cret's other major Texas undertaking was a master plan for the University of Texas in 1930 and the design of a number of the university's buildings, including the 1931 landmark Main Building and Tower which he designed in conjunction with Robert L. White. Local architect Wiley G. Clarkson was Cret's associate on the courthouse. Clarkson, who had recently completed the Classical Moderne-style Masonic Temple and the Zigzag Moderne Sinclair Building, favored historic revival styles, but handled the more progressive Moderne vocabulary with grace and balance. The $1,215,000 building was constructed in 1933 by James I. Barnes Construction Company of Springfield, Ohio, but Barnes complied with a new government policy which required the use of local labor and materials on federal projects whenever they were available.

The five-story courthouse is a sophisticated Classical Moderne building which combines elements of the classical Beaux Arts and Moderne form with elaborate details drawn from Classical, Native American, and Moderne sources. Above the one-story base, the core of the building is defined by a series of three-story convex, black and polished aluminum window panels. Aluminum grilles framing the main entrance doors and freestanding lamps also have rich detailing, including arrows, lotus plant forms, and ziggurat shapes.

Inside, the entrance lobby, which once housed a branch post office and postal savings bank, also featured Moderne decorative motifs. Many of these features were hidden when ceilings were lowered to hide air-conditioning ducts and the space was subdivided for office use. A rehabilitation project undertaken by the General Services Administration Region 7 in 1992-1993 removed the suspended ceiling panels in the lobby and corridor of the first floor to reveal the original ziggurat plaster moldings, uncovered the original terrazzo floors, and restored the marble columns and scrollwork at the courtroom entry.

Upstairs courtrooms have seen fewer alterations than the first floor, and the inlaid wood paneling, suspended bowl-shaped light fixtures, and ceiling moldings remain in place. The fourth-floor U. S. Court of Appeals courtroom contains two murals, "The Taking of Sam Bass" and "Texas Rangers in Camp," painted by Frank Mechau as part of the United States Treasury Department's Section of Fine Arts program which provided works of art for public buildings. These murals are the only examples of Depression-era public art in Fort Worth. ⊛

UNITED STATES COURTHOUSE

UNITED STATES COURTHOUSE

Schools often serve as the focal point for a neighborhood, and the much-beloved Lily B. Clayton Elementary School has held that special place in the hearts of the residents of the Mistletoe Heights and Berkeley neighborhoods for many years. First established in 1918 at the Brite College of the Bible at Texas Christian University as a public school for neighborhood children, the school operated on the TCU campus for almost four years before the new Mistletoe Heights School Building opened on this site on February 17, 1922 with seventy-nine pupils enrolled. The original building, which contained only four classrooms, was designed by Wiley G. Clarkson and built by contractor Harry B. Friedman. The front of the school faced west on Edwin Street, not on Park Place Avenue.

On November 20, 1922, the Fort Worth School Board agreed to name the school for Lily B. Clayton (c. 1863-1942) who taught in the Fort Worth schools from 1885 to 1935. It was the first time that a local school had been named for a living person. Lulu Parker was the first principal and the first woman named to lead a Fort Worth school. The school population increased rapidly as the local neighborhoods developed and, in 1924, four other classrooms were added–two in the basement and two in temporary wooden buildings. By 1932, enrollment had reached 450 students, but the Depression meant that local money for school construction was limited.

A federal Public Works Administration (PWA) program, which provided Fort Worth $4.2 million in loans and grants for construction of thirteen school buildings, made possible the addition which gives Lily B. Clayton its current appearance. Among the schools constructed under this program were North Side Senior High, Arlington Heights Senior High, Polytechnic Senior High, Amon Carter Riverside High, Rosemont Junior High, McLean Junior High, Meadowbrook Elementary, S. S. Dillow Elementary, Oaklawn Elementary, and Morningside Elementary. Architect Preston M. Geren (see also Farrington Field) was selected as the architect for the new addition and for the renovation of the 1922 building. Harry B. Friedman was again selected as the contractor. Geren's design reoriented the front of the building so that it faced Park Place Avenue. The addition, built to the east of the original school, is two stories in height while the older section is only one story, but Geren's facade design covers the Park Place side of the old building so that the expanded school has a uniform appearance.

The new addition, which contains classrooms, an auditorium, library, and offices, was completed in April 1935. The school grounds were landscaped as part of a Works Progress Administration (WPA) program later that year.

Eclectic in design, the school blends elements of Renaissance Revival architecture with decorative detailing from fairy tales. Cast-stone panels on the front and east facades depict Mother Goose, Old Mother Hubbard, Tom Tom the Piper's Son and other characters from children's stories. Inside, the large kindergarten classroom has a working fish pond and a tile mural around the fireplace depicting the story of Peter Rabbit. Other rooms have built-in bookcases and cabinets. Lily B. Clayton was designated as a City of Fort Worth Landmark in 1990. ⊛

LILY B. CLAYTON ELEMENTARY SCHOOL

LILY B. CLAYTON ELEMENTARY SCHOOL

205

*D*espite continued growth on the North Side as a result of the success of the Armour and Swift packing plants, high school students still attended classes at the North Fort Worth High School, 600 Park Avenue, constructed in 1918. By the mid-1930s, conditions were so crowded in the eighteen-room school that wooden out-buildings were used to house overflow classes. Relief came in the form of the federal Public Works Administration (PWA) program.

Several local architects received commissions to design the new school buildings, and Wiley G. Clarkson was selected to draw plans for the North Side Senior High School with the assistance of Charles O. Chromaster. It was the only Moderne-style school building constructed as part of the PWA project. Harry B. Friedman Company, the contractor, built the school at an estimated cost of $459,000.

When it opened on September 13, 1937, the new school almost doubled the amount of classroom space available in the old high school building. There were thirty-three classrooms (including a laboratory, art room, and industrial shops) as well as a gymnasium, library, cafeteria, and auditorium. Situated on a hill overlooking the Jacksboro Highway, the long rectangular cream-colored brick building faces west. The symmetrically balanced facade has classrooms in the middle section with the auditorium on the south end of the building and the gymnasium on the north. Although the original vertical recessed window panels have been replaced in recent years, the overall balance of the building's design, the cast-stone ornamental details (including curling ferns, stepped Mayan designs, and scalloped bands), and the stripes of black brick trim make it an extremely handsome composition. After it opened, the building was repeatedly referred to as one of the most beautiful school buildings in the Southwest.

Inside, terrazzo floors, marble wainscot, mosaic tile columns, decorative plaster moldings, wooden moldings, aluminum balustrades and grilles, and recessed lighting all carry out the Moderne design scheme used on the exterior. The interior has been altered to some degree – most notably changes in the original paint color scheme and lowered ceilings – but it remains an outstanding example of the Moderne style in Fort Worth. ❀

NORTH SIDE SENIOR HIGH SCHOOL

Charles M. Davis (1884-1974) was an engineer who specialized in bridge design, but he carried his interest in concrete construction techniques into other areas by building several Moderne-style concrete houses during the 1930s. Among Davis' major projects were the Universal Mills grain elevators and office building on North Beach Street, the 1918 and 1929 sections of the Ralston Purina Company facility on East Fourth Street, an experimental concrete house constructed at Fair Park in Dallas for the Texas Centennial celebration, and numerous bridges. His own residence, designed by Fort Worth architect Robert P. Woltz, Jr., is unusual among the Period Revival homes that make up its Berkeley Addition neighbors.

After Davis' daughter, Zoe, returned to Fort Worth following studies at Sophie Newcomb College in New Orleans and the Art Students League in New York City, the two began to collaborate on several small, one-bedroom concrete houses that they called "Aparthomes." Idea booklets published by the Portland Cement Association provided the designs for these homes. Although they had intended to sell the houses, the market was not quite ready for such different designs, and the Davises rented the properties for several years.

In 1937, Davis bought the Berkeley Addition lot on which this house now stands and took out a building permit indicating an $11,500 construction cost for the eight-room dwelling. Economical construction was one asset of Davis' homes, which did not require as much finishing work as more traditional houses.

The best of only a handful of Moderne style residences in Fort Worth, Woltz' design may have drawn its inspiration from his work with George Dahl on the 1936 Texas Centennial complex at Fair Park in Dallas. Davis had constructed an experimental concrete residence for the Centennial on behalf of the Portland Cement Association, and it is possible that he and Woltz became interested in each other's work at that time.

Though clearly a vintage design, the house is still strikingly modern in appearance today. Its Streamline Moderne styling draws on an interest in efficient industrial design during the 1930s. Plans in which aerodynamic shapes allowed streams of air to move smoothly over a form were popular, and buildings were designed with the same streamlined shape as planes and ships even though they gained no advantage from such design. The detailing on the Davis House, including the metal-frame windows that wrap around the corners, the ledge or coping at the roofline, the round window and rounded corner above the main door, and the use of glass blocks, is typical of the Streamline Moderne style. ✸

DAVIS HOUSE

*A*nticipating the need for an expanded park system as the result of a rapid increase in population, in 1907 the City of Fort Worth hired noted city planner George Kessler to develop a park plan. One of the areas that Kessler recommended was the site of the current Botanic Garden, which was purchased in 1912. Rock Springs Park was established that same year on a thirty-seven-and-one-half acre tract just west of the Trinity River, a site fed by three natural springs. Little park development took place until the late 1920s, however, because the seller's father retained the right to live on and farm the property.

The Rock Springs area had a varied past. It likely served as a camp site for Indian tribes before the military fort was established. Fort Worth pioneer K. M. Van Zandt (see Van Zandt Cottage) operated a mill here in 1868, and a gravel quarry was located for many years at what is now the eastern end of the rose garden. By the mid-1920s, however, the area was described by one parks official as a "swamp and weed patch."

In November 1925 voters approved a $500,000 bond issue to improve pubic parks. Proposals for Rock Springs Park included a 1929 suggestion by the Tarrant County Rose Society to develop the park as a municipal rose garden and the construction of a water garden area on the east side of the park. Kansas City landscape architect S. Herbert Hare of the firm Hare and Hare drew up the initial plans for the rose garden in February of 1930. Hare was retained by the City of Fort Worth as a consulting landscape architect and his firm, which was a successor to Kessler's operations, designed much of Fort Worth's early park system. The rose garden was inspired by the gardens at Versailles and a small ramp garden at Villa Lante in Bagnaia, Italy.

The Depression was beginning, however, and construction funds were not forthcoming. Riders from nearby stables rode horses in the undeveloped park during the early 1930s, but almost nothing was done in terms of park improvement. In September 1931 the Board of Park Commissioners, an independent body not directly affiliated with the city, gave $15,000 from their budget to city relief, with $7,500 to be spent on Rock Springs Park. City Forester Raymond M. Morrison and work crews made up of men on relief used those funds to lay some stonework on the southern edge of the park near what is now the I-30 frontage road.

When local officials learned that funds were available from the Reconstruction Finance Corporation, a federal relief project headed by Jesse Jones, publisher of the *Houston Chronicle*, the City of Fort Worth and Tarrant County jointly applied for a $340,000 loan to build the rose garden. Their proposal was submitted in October of 1932 and approved in time for construction to begin on February 22, 1933. Hare enlarged his plans – in addition to the rose garden, the project was expanded to include a cactus garden (now a perennial garden) and an arboretum.

The undertaking was the first federal relief project in Fort Worth, and the Botanic Garden has proven to be one of the most enduring and popular attractions in the city. Morrison, who coordinated the project with Tarrant County Rose Society president, Mrs. Ireland Hampton, hired 750 out-of-work stonemasons and apprentices to build the garden. Men who had earned up to $20 per day before the Depression started were now paid $2 per day, sometimes in the form of meal tickets. Nonetheless, they had a great deal of pride in the project which was completed within fifteen months. Approximately 4,000 tons of rock from Palo Pinto County were brought in and used to construct the shelter house, rose ramp, lower garden, colonnade, oval rose garden, and walkways. Queen Tut, the Fort Worth Zoo elephant, was also brought in to aid in the construction effort. When water repeatedly leaked out of the lagoon area, Queen Tut came over from the zoo to wallow and stomp the ground so that it would hold water.

The park was dedicated on October 16, 1933. Though the work on the rose garden grounds was nearly completed, the only roses in sight were cut blooms, as no bushes had been planted. In January 1934 an extra $3,000 became available from the Civil Works Administration, and these funds were used to finish the project. The park commissioners approved a $500 expenditure to purchase both root stock and bushes, and a $75 donation from the men who worked on the garden was used to buy additional roses. The Board of Park Commissioners officially named the area the Fort Worth Botanic Garden on December 18, 1934.

The shelter house at the top of the rose ramp serves as the main entrance to the rose garden. Visitors walk down flanking stone stairways to the rose ramp and lagoon area planted with a variety of water plants or look east to a smaller shelter house (now separated from the garden by University Drive) which was the eastern terminus. At the foot of the rose ramp, a colonnade which serves as an arbor for climbing roses stretches to the north, connecting the main rose garden with a smaller oval rose garden. Hare also designed walking trails, mostly through the wooded areas surrounding the rose garden, which utilized native plants for a naturalistic effect. Before the current University Drive cut through the park, some of these walkways also served as entrance paths.

Although the rose garden, lagoon area, and

wooded portion of the Botanic Garden look much as they did when first constructed, there have been several additions and changes to other parts of the complex through the years. The cactus garden was laid out in 1935, planned by Raymond Morrison according to Herbert Hare's suggestions. That area, north of the shelter and rose ramp, is now a perennial garden. In 1935, the Fort Worth Garden Club was granted permission to use a small structure, originally constructed as a greenhouse and horticulture building in 1934, as a garden center. It was the first such center in Texas. That building has been remodeled and expanded several times, but the original rock structure at the building's core is used as a library and holds the collection given by civic leader Mary Daggett Lake, a member of the Board of Park Commissioners, editor of the Sunday garden page of the *Fort Worth Star-Telegram*, and charter member of the Fort Worth Garden Club.

With the construction of the freeway just to the south of the Botanic Garden during the 1950s, the natural springs dried up. Water for the park is now pumped in from the nearby Trinity River. Over the years, additional acreage has been added to the garden, and it is now a 114-acre park with a number of specialty garden areas. In 1970, a Japanese Garden was constructed in an old rock quarry north of the garden center building, and in 1985-1986, a new conservatory building was built at the north end of the garden. The Fort Worth Botanic Garden is still a favorite place for weddings, family reunions, picnics, or quiet walks. ❀

FORT WORTH BOTANIC GARDEN

FORT WORTH BOTANIC GARDEN/ROSE RAMP

FORT WORTH BOTANIC GARDEN

213

$\mathcal{E}$rvin Stanley Farrington, long-time athletic director for the Fort Worth public schools, dreamed of a new public school athletic stadium but died in November 1937 while the facility was still in the planning stages. By the time ground was broken on March 10, 1938, the decision had been made to name the stadium for Farrington.

Construction of the 20,000-seat stadium was a cooperative project between the Works Progress Administration (WPA) and the Fort Worth school district. The school system purchased the thirty-eight-acre tract on which the stadium sits from the City of Fort Worth. Project costs were to be shared – the government contributed $160,000 in federal funds from the WPA and the school district provided $84,000. Labor was provided by WPA workers, and newspaper accounts estimated that the project would employ between 400 and 550 men for six to eight months.

The stadium was designed by local architect Preston M. Geren's office. According to Fort Worth architectural historian Judith Singer Cohen, Geren's designers Arthur George King and Everett L. Frazier actually produced the designs for the stadium. Gravel for the concrete structure was dug from the site. Work progressed slowly, and the stadium did not open until September 1939.

The Classical Moderne stadium contained not only the football field and a 220-yard straight-away track but dressing rooms, offices, and a ninety-foot press box with space for forty-five reporters and two broadcasting booths. The seventy-foot tall square fluted piers on the stadium's west facade, the bas relief panels of athletes by Fort Worth artist Evaline Sellors (c. 1904-1995), the lettering and other stylized trim are hallmarks of the Classical Moderne style. During the mid-1980s, an attempt was made to demolish the stadium and build a hotel and retail complex on the site, but a reverter clause in the deed, which would have returned the land to the City of Fort Worth if it were not used for recreational purposes, stopped the plan. The stadium continues to serve the Fort Worth Independent School District as an athletic facility. ⊗

FARRINGTON FIELD

FARRINGTON FIELD

216

FARRINGTON FIELD

$\mathcal{F}$ort Worth, like many other communities, utilized federal relief funds to upgrade its civic infrastructure during the Depression. In the case of the 1938 City Hall, the Public Works Administration (PWA) provided approximately forty-five per cent of the $500,000 construction cost, and the balance was funded by a city bond issue. Fort Worth's old Victorian city hall, constructed in 1892-1893, was felt by many to be outmoded. Both social reformers and the business community worked for the passage of the bond election that made construction of this building and a library (sadly, demolished in 1991) possible. The 1893 Victorian city hall was demolished so that the site could be used for this building, and construction began in December 1937.

Wyatt C. Hedrick and the Elmer G. Withers Architectural Company were the project architects. Herman Paul Koeppe, Hedrick's chief designer, was responsible for much of the building's design including a number of proposed interior murals and other decorative details that were never executed due to financial problems. James T. Taylor was the contractor. His firm finished the building in approximately thirteen months, and the first city council meeting was held in the new structure on January 4, 1939.

The Classical or "PWA" Moderne building is four stories tall with a full basement and sub-basement. In the words of Walter A. Koons, regional counsel for the PWA who spoke at the dedication, it is "sturdy, unpretentious, yet impressive." Constructed of reinforced concrete sheathed in Texas cream-colored Cordova limestone, it has an entrance portico of Minnesota black granite with aluminum windows, doors, and grilles. The building reflects a machine-age aesthetic–an appreciation for the amount of efficient work that machines could do and the streamlined form of mechanical design–in the style of the decorative aluminum grilles on the front facade.

Inside, the building has a dark pink marble wainscot, terrazzo floors, fluted moldings, and frosted-glass-and-aluminum light fixtures. When it opened the building had no furniture, and one of the first acts that the city council took in its new meeting space was to authorize a $23,438.50 contract for furnishings. Despite the financial constraints which did not allow some of Koeppe's key design elements to be carried out, the building is a handsome and dignified Moderne composition that reflects both the civic pride and financial struggle of this period of Fort Worth's history.

When it first opened, the sub-basement housed the boiler and store rooms, while the police department was located in the basement. The water and tax departments were on the first floor. City council chambers, municipal court, and administrative offices were on the second floor, while department heads officed on the third floor; and the health department occupied the fourth floor. Most city offices were located here through the 1960s, including the police department and jail. After the current city hall was completed in 1971, this building was renamed the Public Safety and Courts Building. It currently houses the city's municipal court and other departmental offices. ⊛

CITY HALL/PUBLIC SAFETY AND COURTS BUILDING

CITY HALL/PUBLIC SAFETY AND COURTS BUILDING

CITY HALL/PUBLIC SAFETY AND COURTS BUILDING

WILL ROGERS MEMORIAL CENTER

*A*mon G. Carter thought that either San Antonio or Houston, cities with historic ties to the 1836 revolution, would be chosen as the site of the 1936 Texas Centennial celebration. When Dallas, a city which he felt had little going for it besides money, was chosen, Carter and a group of Fort Worth businessmen decided that Fort Worth should have a piece of the action. After an initial request to the federal Public Works Administration for funds to construct a coliseum and auditorium to be used for the Centennial celebration and livestock shows (dubbed "Amon's cowshed" by its detractors) was turned down, Carter appealed to President Franklin Delano Roosevelt. Federal funding became available for the project in November of 1935. With supplemental funds from a City of Fort Worth bond issue and local donations, promoters were eventually able to construct the coliseum, auditorium, and tower as well as several permanent exhibit buildings and a temporary entertainment complex (including the 1936 Casa Manana, Pioneer Palace, and Jumbo–a circus arena) to house the Fort Worth Frontier Centennial festivities.

The projected cost of the three main structures–the coliseum, auditorium, and tower–was $975,000. It was originally hoped that these facilities might be ready in time for the Centennial celebration, and the project was put on the fast track. The firms of Wyatt C. Hedrick, Architect-Engineers, and Elmer G. Withers Architectural Company were selected to design the project. Herman Paul Koeppe was responsible for the design work on the coliseum and tower, while engineer Herbert M. Hinckley, Sr. (1897-1938), devised the innovative structural plans for the coliseum's dome which allowed an unobstructed interior view through the use of arched trusses joined at a monitor ridge. Donald S. Nelson, who worked with Withers, was responsible for the auditorium design. On December 18, 1935, the City of Fort Worth bought 138 acres of land west of the Trinity River and east of the Arlington Heights neighborhood from the K. M. Van Zandt Land Company. Excavation and foundation contracts for all three facilities were awarded on February 10, 1936, to Butcher and Sweeney, and ground was broken on March 10, exactly one month later. Construction contracts, awarded later in March, went to R. F. Ball Construction Company for the auditorium and tower and to James T. Taylor and Company for the coliseum. By the time the Frontier Centennial opened in July, the temporary buildings were ready, but the coliseum, auditorium, and tower were still under construction.

Even though the Centennial celebration was officially over by the time the buildings were completed late in 1936, these structures proved their "civic usefulness." In 1944, the Southwestern Exposition and Fat Stock Show (now called the Southwestern Exposition and Livestock Show) moved to the Will Rogers complex from the North Side Coliseum. In addition to the stock show, which attracts thousands of visitors each year, the coliseum has been the site of a variety of equestrian events, conventions, circuses, boxing matches, religious revivals, and ice shows. For its part, the auditorium has hosted countless high school graduations, concerts, and theatrical productions. It is appropriate that the complex, located in Fort Worth's cultural district near the Kimbell Art Museum, Amon Carter Museum, Museum of Science and History, and Museum of Modern Art, draws events reflecting the city's rich and diverse heritage.

Flanking the Pioneer Tower, the buff-yellow brick veneered coliseum and auditorium have similar curving facades fronted by massive fluted limestone piers. Above the piers, tile friezes or mural-scale panels depict people and events in the history of Texas. The friezes were designed by Koeppe with the assistance of Kenneth Gale of the Mosaic Tile Company of Zanesville, Ohio, the firm which produced and assembled the glazed tile panels.

Inside, the coliseum is the more ornate of the two buildings. Stylized Art Deco ceiling paintings, sunburst-form aluminum balustrades, glass-block windows, frosted glass light fixtures, rows of square fluted columns and piers, terrazzo floors, and Monel plaques featuring agricultural and rodeo motifs on the end of the balcony walls adorn the lobby, while the arena has a more utilitarian design.

The auditorium, which was the city's first municipal auditorium, has an almost austere lobby with fossil shellstone walls, a black and white-striped terrazzo floor, and a geometric-design ceiling panel. The auditorium itself has minimal decoration with six decorative metal screens and masks representing Comedy and Tragedy flanking the stage. The original plans called for additional embellishments, but funding did not allow their execution.

The Pioneer Tower, a soaring brick-and-stone column with an octagonal, stair-stepped aluminum crown, is a West Side landmark. Glass-block panels on the side of the tower were originally lit at night, but they have been covered with metal louvers and no longer complement the still-functioning crown lighting. Inside the rotunda, fluted classical columns, decorative grilles, and pyramidal light fixtures provide a backdrop for four large metal plaques honoring early Texas settlers. A pedestal in the center of the rotunda holds a bust of the complex's namesake, Will Rogers, who was a close friend of Amon Carter. After Rogers died in a 1935 Alaska airplane crash, Carter determined to honor Rogers by naming the complex for him.

In July 1990, a City of Fort Worth bond program which would have provided funds to preserve the coliseum and auditorium facades while erecting a new performance hall in place of the old auditorium failed. Supporters felt that deferred maintenance and spatial constraints made the original auditorium unusable, arguing that a new hall behind the old facade was the only way to provide a facility that could be used by the symphony, ballet, opera, and other performing groups. Opponents believed strongly that all of the historic auditorium should be preserved and felt that it could be rehabilitated, making the hall useful for a limited number of groups at a smaller overall cost, which would translate into lower rental fees. Several months after the bond issue failed, city inspectors found unacceptable levels of asbestos in the auditorium's ventilation system and closed the building. Using bond funds approved for renovation in a previous election, the city rehabilitated the auditorium and reopened it for public use on May 31, 1992. Lee Roy Hahnfeld was the project architect, and construction work was handled by The DeMoss Company.

The Will Rogers complex has served Fort Worth and Texas for almost sixty years. Several expansions, including stock show barns built between 1935 and 1955, the 1984 Amon Carter Exhibit Hall, and the world-class Equestrian Center constructed in 1987-1988 have increased the facility's usefulness while maintaining its rich architectural and historical traditions. ✾

WILL ROGERS MEMORIAL COLISEUM

WILL ROGERS MEMORIAL COLISEUM

225

WILL ROGERS MEMORIAL COLISEUM

$\mathcal{S}$UGGESTED READINGS

Readers seeking additional information about Fort Worth's historic buildings, the architectural styles that were favored, and the community's history may wish to consult one or more of the following sources. Out-of-print books may be found in many area libraries or borrowed through an inter-library loan request.

Judith Singer Cohen's *Cowtown Moderne* (College Station: Texas A & M University Press, 1989; out of print) is an award-winning account of the Art Deco and Moderne buildings constructed in Fort Worth during the 1920s and 1930s. Richly illustrated with both historic and contemporary photographs, Cohen's book provides detailed architectural descriptions, historical background about the period when the buildings were constructed, and biographical information about the architects.

The *Tarrant County Historic Resources Survey* (Fort Worth: Historic Preservation Council for Tarrant County, various dates; some volumes out of print) was the project which originally led to the idea for this book. During the late 1970s, local preservationists recognized the need to evaluate and document the county's historic buildings so that preservation strategies could be organized. Conducted over a ten-year period, the survey identified over 2,200 resources (buildings and objects such as bridges, monuments, and brick streets) of architectural and historical significance. The results were published in several volumes, each covering a geographic region of the county. Each entry has an illustration of the resource and a brief architectural and historical description. The volumes which cover Fort Worth buildings include: Fort Worth Central Business District (1991), Fort Worth Southside (1986; out of print), Fort Worth Near North Side, West Side * Westover Hills (1988), Fort Worth Upper North, Northeast, East, Far South and Far West (1989), and Selected Tarrant County Communities (1990). For additional information about how the buildings were selected for this volume, please see the preface.

Virginia and Lee McAlester's *A Field Guide to American Houses* (New York: Alfred A. Knopf, 1986) contains an excellent analysis of American house styles.

Identifying American Architecture: A Pictorial Guide to the Styles and Terms, 1600-1945 (Nashville: American Association for State and Local History, rev. ed. 1981) by John J.-G. Blumenson discusses commercial, civic, and residential buildings and has a useful glossary of architectural terms.

Produced by the National Trust for Historic Preservation, *What Style is It?* by John S. Poppeliers, Allen Chambers, and Nancy B. Schwartz (Washington: Preservation Press, 1983) offers a good overview of historic American building styles.

GENERAL FORT WORTH HISTORIES

Fort Worth: Outpost on the Trinity (Norman: University of Oklahoma Press, 1953, out of print; and Fort Worth: TCU Press, 1990) by Oliver Knight and Julia Kathryn Garrett's *Fort Worth: A Frontier Triumph* (Austin: Encino Press, 1972; out of print) both deal at length with Fort Worth's nineteenth century history. TCU Press added an essay by Cissy Stewart Lale about twentieth-century events to Oliver Knight's volume when it reprinted the book in 1990.

Three books: Leonard Sanders, *How Fort Worth Became the Texasmost City, 1849-1920* (Fort Worth: Amon Carter Museum, 1973, out of print; and reprint edition, Fort Worth: TCU Press, 1986); Caleb Pirtle, *Fort Worth: The Civilized West* (Tulsa: Continental Heritage Press, 1980; out of print); and Janet Schmelzer, *Where the West Begins: Fort Worth and Tarrant County* (Northridge, California: Windsor Publications, 1985; out of print) are illustrated histories, reproducing many historic photographs. Sanders' book was prepared in conjunction with an exhibition at the Amon Carter Museum, and Pirtle and Schmelzer's volumes contain business history sections which profile local companies.

Other books on specific areas of Fort Worth history include J'Nell Pate's *Livestock Legacy: The Fort Worth Stockyards 1887-1987* (College Station: Texas A & M University Press, 1988) and *North of the River: A Brief History of North Fort Worth* (Fort Worth: TCU Press, 1994) which deal with the north side and livestock industry; Richard F. Selcer's account of *Hell's Half Acre: The Life and Legend of a Red-Light District* (Fort Worth: TCU Press, 1991); and *Oil Legends of Fort Worth*, compiled by the Petroleum Club of Fort Worth (Fort Worth: Petroleum Club, 1993) which profiles many of Fort Worth's most prominent oilmen.

INDEX

Main entries for each building are in bold type.